THE 66 BOOKS OF THE BIBLE

The 66 Books of the Bible

Norman Owen

THE CHRISTADELPHIAN
404 SHAFTMOOR LANE
BIRMINGHAM B28 8SZ

2007

First published 1997
Reprinted 1998, 2002, 2007

ISBN 978–085189140–8

Printed by The Cromwell Press
Trowbridge, Wiltshire, UK

Preface

THE Bible speaks with supreme authority. Every part is from God. All its writers were directly inspired by Him. So the sixty-six books form one powerful, consistent message from Heaven!

Many threads interweave to form this Book of inestimable beauty and worth. Nothing can compare with the Divine pattern in this priceless treasure. The Bible is perfect and complete; nothing can surpass it.

The Bible carries conviction. It is true to life, honest about our human nature. Not one of its historical records has ever been proved wrong. Its amazing prophecies are still coming true. Its message for the world and for individuals remains the only bright light in a darkening age. Read it in humility—it will bring you hope and ultimate joy!

NORMAN OWEN

Bible Versions

Most quotations from the Scriptures are from the Authorised (King James) Version, but occasionally the wording of the Revised Version is followed; or the text of the Revised Standard Version (RSV), New International Version (NIV) or New King James Version (NKJV) is used.

Acknowledgements

THE chapters of this book first appeared as articles in the magazine *Glad Tidings* and it was the initiative of the editor of that magazine which led to the work being offered for publication in book form. The material lent itself ideally to the format of the Study Guide series; and readers who have enjoyed the Study Guides will find this new addition to the series—alongside the Scriptures themselves—a valuable aid to Bible exploration. The rather larger format has made it possible to amplify the original articles, while extra pages have been added to introduce each new section of the Bible.

The publishers express warm thanks to the following whose illustrations have been incorporated: Phyllis Vincent (sheaf of corn, page 12); Paul Harrison (David and Goliath, page 13); Stanley Owen (sketches on page 31, taken from his *Song of Solomon Study Guide*); Paul Wasson (several sketches and all the maps) and Angela Willis (a number of line drawings and charts). Other drawings are the author's, or are taken from non-copyright sources. For the chronology of the Judges we are indebted to Maurice Beale.

The book is commended to all in the trust that the work of God Himself, the Divine Author of the inspired Scriptures, will be acknowledged as a result of the reading of these pages.

Contents

HOW WE GOT OUR BIBLE

God inspired the Old Testament writers

בראשית
GENESIS.

The opening verses of Genesis

Hebrew Old Testament

KATA MAΘΘAION

God inspired the New Testament writers

The opening verses of Matthew

Greek New Testament

Papyrus manuscript of 2 Corinthians 1:1-8

In 1947 some very ancient Hebrew scrolls were found in the caves of Qumran near the Dead Sea

The English Bible

Wycliffe (1382)
Tyndale (1525)
The Great Bible (1539)
Geneva Bible (1560)
Authorised (King James) Version (1611)
Revised Version (1885)
Revised Standard Version (1952)
New English Bible (1970)
New International Version (1978)
New King James Version (1982)

Foreign Language Bibles

German
Spanish
French
Esperanto
Swahili
Russian
Korean …

… a total of over 2,000 languages

"No prophecy of Scripture is of any private interpretation, for prophecy never came by the will of man, but holy men of God spoke as they were moved by the Holy Spirit." (2 Peter 1:20)

Every year more than 20 million Bibles in the English language are printed

DIVISIONS OF THE BIBLE

66 Great Books from God—"All Scripture is given by inspiration of God" (2 Timothy 3:16)

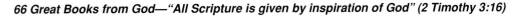

THE BIBLE is really one book, whose author is the Lord God. 'The Good Book', as it has been called, is God's Guide Book to Life—for all to read. Without it, we shall wander aimlessly through life, to the grave. With it, we can know what God has in store for the earth, and how we can share in His glorious purpose, centred in the Lord Jesus Christ. The twin themes of both Old and New Testaments (see Acts 8:12) are:
- The Kingdom of God
- Jesus Christ

Old Testament

History

1 Genesis
2 Exodus
3 Leviticus
4 Numbers
5 Deuteronomy
6 Joshua
7 Judges
8 Ruth

Every part of the Bible matters. The wonderful links between these 66 Books become apparent when you read from all sections of God's Word, humbly and prayerfully.

9 1 Samuel
10 2 Samuel
11 1 Kings
12 2 Kings
13 1 Chronicles
14 2 Chronicles
15 Ezra
16 Nehemiah
17 Esther

Poetry

18 Job
19 Psalms
20 Proverbs
21 Ecclesiastes
22 Song of Solomon

Prophecy

23 Isaiah
24 Jeremiah
25 Lamentations
26 Ezekiel
27 Daniel
28 Hosea
29 Joel
30 Amos
31 Obadiah
32 Jonah
33 Micah
34 Nahum
35 Habakkuk
36 Zephaniah
37 Haggai
38 Zechariah
39 Malachi

New Testament

Gospels and Acts

40 Matthew
41 Mark
42 Luke
43 John
44 Acts of the Apostles

Letters

45 Romans
46 1 Corinthians
47 2 Corinthians
48 Galatians
49 Ephesians
50 Philippians
51 Colossians
52 1 Thessalonians
53 2 Thessalonians
54 1 Timothy
55 2 Timothy
56 Titus
57 Philemon
58 Hebrews
59 James
60 1 Peter
61 2 Peter
62 1 John
63 2 John
64 3 John
65 Jude

Prophecy

66 Revelation

Map of Old Testament Times

Some of the places and peoples associated with the history of Israel and God's purpose.

For the following, see maps on the pages indicated:

(Other maps specific to the prophets are featured on pages 38, 39, 42, 43, 44, 45, 46, 48)

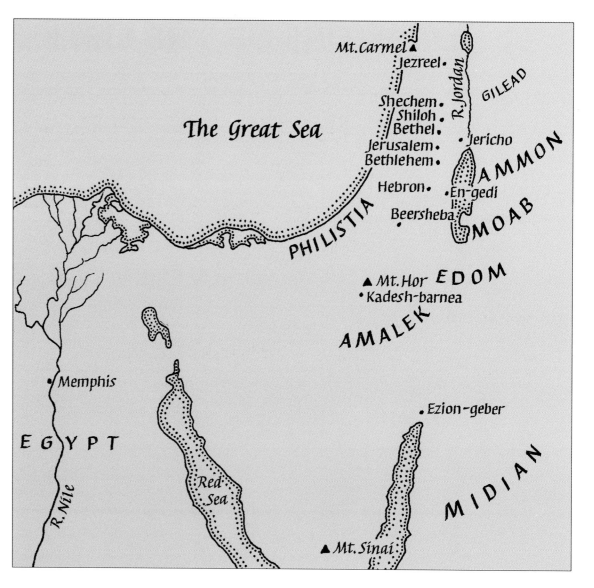

Mt. Carmel ▲
Jezreel •
R. Jordan
GILEAD
The Great Sea
Shechem •
Shiloh •
Bethel •
Jerusalem •
Bethlehem •
• Jericho
AMMON
Hebron •
• En-gedi
PHILISTIA
Beersheba •
MOAB
▲ Mt. Hor
EDOM
• Kadesh-barnea
AMALEK
• Memphis
• Ezion-geber
EGYPT
Red Sea
MIDIAN
R. Nile
▲ Mt. Sinai

HISTORY SECTION

"He made known his ways unto Moses,
His acts unto the children of Israel."
(Psalm 103:7)

Books 1-17

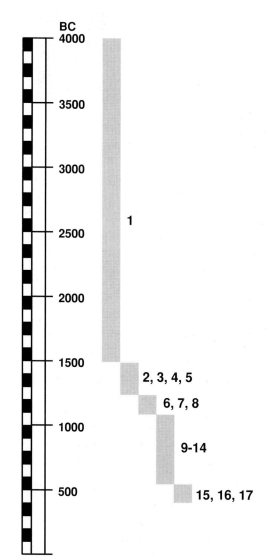

BC

Introduction to the
HISTORY SECTION

No.	Book	Contents
1 2 3 4 5	Genesis Exodus Leviticus Numbers Deuteronomy	THE PENTATEUCH (5 BOOKS) A history of God's dealings with early man, His promises to Abraham and His work with Israel, the people He brought out from Egypt
6 7 8	Joshua Judges Ruth	THE EARLY SETTLEMENT OF ISRAEL IN THE PROMISED LAND
9 10 11 12 13 14	1 Samuel 2 Samuel 1 Kings 2 Kings 1 Chronicles 2 Chronicles	THE KINGDOM OF GOD IN ISRAEL A history of the Kings and Prophets in God's Kingdom, from the time of Samuel until the overthrow of Jerusalem and the captivity of the Jews in Babylon
15 16 17	Ezra Nehemiah Esther	AFTER THE CAPTIVITY

PEOPLE MENTIONED IN GENESIS

ADAM—Eve

Cain Abel SETH

NOAH

SHEM Ham Japheth

ABRAHAM—Sarah

Ishmael ISAAC

Esau JACOB (ISRAEL)

Reuben Levi Judah Joseph

Manasseh Ephraim

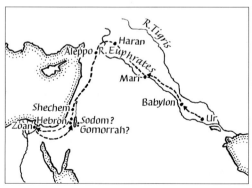

Abraham's Journeys

GENESIS

1

The name "Genesis" means 'birth' or 'beginning'. In this book we learn about very important beginnings in God's plan for the Earth.

"In the beginning God created the heaven and the earth" (1:1). The opening words of the Bible teach that God is the Creator of the universe, which He made with a plan and a purpose.

A Book of Beginnings

- The beginning of life on earth (chs 1-2)
- The origin of sin and death and the promise of a Saviour (ch 3)
- The Flood: a new beginning with Noah's family, saved in the ark (chs 6-10)
- Babel: the origin of languages and races of mankind (ch 11)
- The beginnings of Israel (chs 12-32)

God called Abraham and his family to leave Ur, in Mesopotamia, to migrate to "a land that I will show thee" (12:1)—Canaan, the future land of promise. Lot, his nephew, settled near Sodom and Gomorrah, and had to be rescued when those evil cities were destroyed.

God's Promises through Abraham

God promised Abraham: **(a)** a "seed" (Jesus Christ)—Isaac was a child of promise in the short term, but the "seed" promised to Abraham (22:17; Galatians 3:16) was Christ; **(b)** a nation—God's people, in the first place Israel (17:7-8), but extended to those who are "in Christ" (Galatians 3:29); **(c)** inheritance of the promised land of Israel by the faithful; **(d)** blessings for all nations—"In thee shall all families of the earth be blessed" (12:3).

Abraham's faith was tested when God asked him to slay Isaac. He had the knife poised but his hand was stayed, and "in a figure" Abraham received his son back from the dead (Hebrews 11:17-19). The promises were repeated to Isaac (26:3) and Jacob (28:13), whose name was changed to Israel. Jacob had twelve sons, heads of the twelve tribes of Israel.

Jacob's sons sell Joseph into Egypt as a slave, but he is promoted to be Pharaoh's prime minister! Jacob and his family join Joseph in Egypt, but Jacob (47:30) and Joseph (50:24,25) both ask to be buried in the promised land of Israel.

Some interesting links with other parts of the Bible

For example: *Compared with:*

a) Genesis 2:7	a) 1 Corinthians 15:45
b) Genesis 2:24	b) Matthew 19:4,5
c) Genesis 13:15	c) Galatians 3:16-29
d) Genesis 15:7	d) Acts 7:5

5

2

EXODUS

The record of how the Israelites were saved out of Egypt, led through the Sinai Desert for 40 years and brought to the borders of Canaan.

A Way Out

The word "Exodus" means 'a going out'. The first part of the Book of Exodus contains the record of how God made a *way out* for His people Israel. He chose Moses to be their leader. Then, after ten mighty plagues against Egypt and its gods, and other miracles such as the drying up of the sea to let them cross, He took them out of the slavery of Egypt, to go to the Promised Land. The rest of the Book of Exodus records their journeyings in the Sinai desert.

The Wilderness Wanderings

Great Events

Among the great miraculous events recorded in Exodus are:

1. The Burning Bush—ch 3
2. The 10 Plagues—chs 7-12
3. The Passover—chs 12-13
4. Crossing the Red Sea—chs 13-15
5. Bread from Heaven—ch 16
6. Water from the Rock—ch 17
7. Israel at Mount Sinai—ch 19
8. The giving of the Law (including the ten commandments)—chs 20-31
9. Incident of the Golden Calf—ch 32
10. Making and erecting the Tabernacle, where God's glory came to dwell (see plan)—chs 25-40

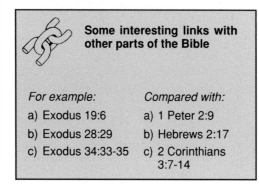

Some interesting links with other parts of the Bible

For example:	Compared with:
a) Exodus 19:6	a) 1 Peter 2:9
b) Exodus 28:29	b) Hebrews 2:17
c) Exodus 34:33-35	c) 2 Corinthians 3:7-14

PLAGUES AND EGYPTIAN GODS

Plague	Directed Against
Nile turned to Blood	Hapi, Khnum, Osiris (gods of the Nile)
Cattle Plague	Hathor (cow goddess), Mnevis and Apis (sacred bulls)
Darkness	Ra, Aten, Atmu (sun gods)

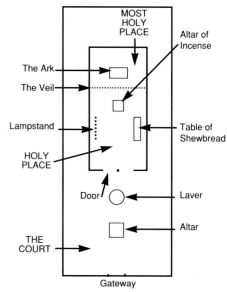

The Tabernacle (Exodus 32-40)

LEVITICUS

3

God's laws given to Israel at Sinai: details of the sacrifices and the personal and collective life of holiness required of Israel.

FEAST DAYS AND THEIR PROPHETIC SIGNIFICANCE

MONTHS	FEASTS	FUTURE
1 APR	Passover	Death of Jesus
2 MAY		
3 JUN	Firstfruits (start of harvest)	Christ and his followers
4 JUL		
5 AUG		
6 SEP	Trumpets	Return of Israel
7 OCT	Atonement	Repentance of Israel
8 NOV	Tabernacles (harvest complete)	Kingdom Age
9 DEC		
10 JAN		
11 FEB		
12 MAR		

Priesthood

Aaron (of the tribe of Levi) was Israel's first High Priest. His sons and descendants continued the priesthood over the next eight centuries. Though the Levitical priesthood failed, through disobedience, God would later provide a "better priesthood": Jesus Christ (of the tribe of Judah) is the only priest today, a mediator between God and men (1 Timothy 2:5).

Christ and the Offerings

Jesus Christ perfectly fulfilled all that was intended in the various offerings. His total dedication and sinlessness made him the perfect offering for those who look in faith to God for atonement (see Hebrews 10).

OFFERINGS UNDER THE LAW

Offering	Ref.	Meaning
BURNT	ch 1	Giving self to God
MEAL	ch 2	Thanks to God
PEACE	ch 3	Peace with God
SIN	ch 4	Sinful nature
TRESPASS	ch 5	Personal sins
ATONEMENT	ch 16	National cleansing

Some interesting links with other parts of the Bible

For example:
a) Leviticus 10:3
b) Leviticus 17:11
c) Leviticus 23:39,40

Compared with:
a) Isaiah 52:11; 1 Peter 1:15,16
b) Hebrews 9:22
c) Hosea 12:9; Zechariah 14:16

The High Priest

7

NUMBERS

Incidents in the wilderness, following Israel's faithless failure, which prevented their entry into the Promised Land.

The Book of Numbers is so called because it records two censuses or 'numberings' of the Israelites:

1 At Sinai—1:1-3

2 Near to Canaan—ch 26

Forty Long Years

The 12 spies sent to reconnoitre in the Promised Land (ch 13) reported that the Canaanite cities were highly fortified and their armies powerful. Presented with this news, Israel lost faith in God's promise to give them the Land.

So for another 38 years they had to wander in the deserts. Their journeyings, especially during the final years, are related in chs 21-36. All the generation which left Egypt (from 20 years old and upwards) died in the desert, except some of the faithful Levites, and Joshua and Caleb, the only two spies who showed faith in God.

Chapter Summary

1st Census	ch 1
The Camp	ch 2
Levites	ch 4
Nazarites	ch 6
Princes	ch 8
Order of marching	ch 10
Taberah	ch 11
Miriam's revolt	ch 12
Spies' report	ch 13
Korah's revolt	ch 16
Water from the rock	ch 20
Fiery Serpents	ch 21
Balaam's prophecies	chs 22-24
2nd Census	ch 26
Various laws and feasts	chs 28-30
List of journeys	chs 33-34

(LACK OF FAITH — from Taberah to Fiery Serpents)

Numbers (ch 1) according to Tribe
(Men over 20 and excluding Levi)

Reuben 46,500	Ephraim 40,500
Simeon 59,300	Manasseh 32,200
Gad............45,650	Benjamin 35,400
Judah..........74,600	Dan..............62,700
Issachar 54,400	Asher 41,500
Zebulun.......57,400	Naphtali 53,400

Total 603,550

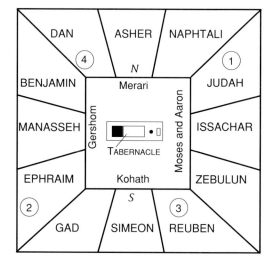

The 12 tribes (4 standards) encamped around the Tabernacle and its priesthood, during the wilderness journeyings (Numbers 2). For explanation of the standards, see page 58 (Mark)

Some interesting links with other parts of the Bible

For example:
a) Numbers 14:21
b) Numbers 21:8-9
c) Numbers 24:17

Compared with:
a) Isaiah 11:9; Habakkuk 2:14
b) John 3:14-15; 2 Corinthians 5:21
c) Genesis 49:10; Psalm 110:2

DEUTERONOMY

Phylactery

5

A new generation of Israelites, journeying in the wilderness, had God's laws repeated to them as they neared the borders of the Promised Land.

A New Generation

Forty years had passed since God brought Israel out from Egypt by a series of great miracles. He had since wonderfully provided for them during their wanderings in the Sinai peninsula.

In Deuteronomy (which means 'repeating the Law') we read how God reminded the new generation of His acts as they now stood near the borders of the Promised Land. God pleads with them to be more faithful than their fathers had been.

Remember the Days of Old

Chs 1-10 contain a review of what God had already done for His people, from Egypt onwards. They were exhorted to learn from the lessons of the past. We too should learn that these things are written for our eternal benefit (see Romans 15:4).

In the Mind

In later years, Jews sometimes wore little boxes containing Scripture texts on parchment, called 'phylacteries', which they fastened on their foreheads or arms. What really matters, is to have the Word of God in our minds (see Deuteronomy 6:6; Matthew 23:5; Hebrews 8:10).

Remember God's Word

There is an emphasis in Deuteronomy on the need to remember (see 4:9; 6:12; 8:2,11,18; 9:7; 11:18; 32:7).

Jesus remembered God's Word; it was deeply impressed on his mind. Thus he was strengthened against the temptations which arose from within. When, in the wilderness, three such temptations came (Matthew 4:1-10), they were quickly rebuffed with words from God's Book—all three were met with quotations remembered from Deuteronomy (8:3; 6:16; 10:20)! In the same way God's Word in our minds can help us overcome temptation.

The Jews—God's Chosen People

"The LORD did not set his love upon you, nor choose you, because ye were more in number than any people; for ye were the fewest of all people: but because the LORD loved you, and because he would keep the oath which he had sworn unto your fathers, hath the LORD brought you out with a mighty hand, and redeemed you out of the house of bondmen, from the hand of Pharaoh king of Egypt."

Deuteronomy 7:7,8

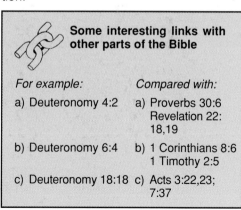

Some interesting links with other parts of the Bible

For example:	Compared with:
a) Deuteronomy 4:2	a) Proverbs 30:6 Revelation 22:18,19
b) Deuteronomy 6:4	b) 1 Corinthians 8:6 1 Timothy 2:5
c) Deuteronomy 18:18	c) Acts 3:22,23; 7:37

JOSHUA

The Divine record of the conquest of Canaan under Joshua, and the subsequent division of the Land among the twelve tribes of Israel.

The Lord's Servant

Joshua had been a captain of Israel's army (Exodus 17:9,10) and a personal servant to Moses (Exodus 24:13). After the death of Moses, God chose Joshua to lead His people into the Promised Land. Now, as God's servant, he must be "strong and very courageous" (1:1-9).

Preparing the Way

Two spies were sent ahead to the Canaanite fortress of Jericho (ch 2). Then, by a miracle, the River Jordan—which was in flood—was parted so that the Israelites could cross over (ch 3).

On the West Bank, Israel encamped at Gilgal which became a temporary headquarters during the campaigns which followed. The Passover was kept (ch 5) and the people prepared for battle.

Early Conquests

The overthrow of Jericho by Divine power (ch 6) was followed by the conquest of Ai (ch 8), cities in the South (ch 10) and cities in the North (ch 11) (see campaign routes on map).

After 7 years the occupation of the Land was complete. The 12 tribes were given their portions and the Levites and Priests were allotted 48 cities throughout the country. Six "cities of refuge" were appointed to which those who had accidentally committed manslaughter could flee (ch 20; see Numbers 35:9-34).

Joshua and Jesus

Joshua was a pointer to Jesus. The two names are virtually the same and mean 'God saves'. As Joshua, with God's help, conquered the enemy, so Jesus conquered sin.

Some interesting links with other parts of the Bible

For example:

a) Joshua 1:6

b) Joshua 2:1; 6:17-23

c) Joshua 18:1

Compared with:

a) Genesis 15:18-21; 26:3

b) Hebrews 11:31; James 2:25

c) Jeremiah 7:12; Acts 7:45

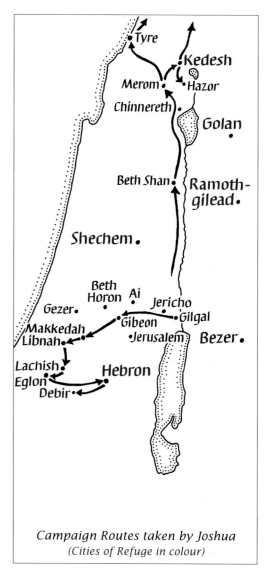

Campaign Routes taken by Joshua
(Cities of Refuge in colour)

APPROXIMATE CHRONOLOGY
(some dates are uncertain)

BC

1447 Exodus

1400

1407 Conquest/Joshua

1346 **Othniel** (ch 3)

1300

1288 **Ehud** (ch 3)
Shamgar (ch 3)
1260 **Deborah**/Barak (chs 4,5)

1213 **Gideon** (chs 6-8)

1200

1173 Abimelech   1170 **Tola** (ch 10)

1147 **Jair** (ch 10)

1107 **Jephthah** (ch 11) 1101 **Ibzon** (ch 12)
1094 **Elon** (ch 12)
1084 **Abdon** (ch 12)

1100

1064 Eli

1044 **Samson** (chs 13-16)
Samuel

1023 Saul
1011 David

1000

JUDGES

7

A history of the period during which God saved the largely disobedient Israel from surrounding nations, by the hand of certain tribal leaders called 'judges'

No King in Israel

The Book of Judges covers the period from the death of Joshua to the time of Samuel (see chart and Acts 13:20).

During this time Israel often failed to look to God as their Ruler—hence the repeated comment: "In those days there was no king in Israel" (18:1; 19:1; 21:25).

The Judges

Many times during this period surrounding nations were able to invade Israel (see map). However, from time to time, God gave Israel deliverers—the judges—who, with His help, overcame those enemies and ruled God's people.

Jesus the Judge

When reading this book, it is profitable to look for comparisons with Jesus Christ— the One sent by God to save His people from sin and death, who will come again to Israel as Judge, Deliverer and King (see Interesting Links below).

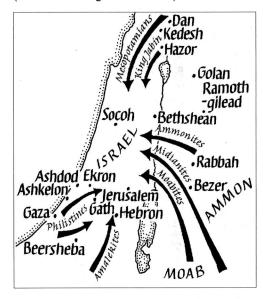

Some interesting links with other parts of the Bible

For example: *Compared with:*

a) Judges 5:12   a) Psalm 68:18; Ephesians 4:8

b) Judges 8:23   b) John 6:15

c) Judges 11:27   c) Genesis 18:25; Matthew 25:34; Acts 17:30,31

RUTH

The record of the Moabitess who turned to Israel's God, married Boaz of Bethlehem and became an ancestor of Jesus Christ!

Bethlehem

Time of the Judges

The events in this lovely little book, only four chapters long, took place in the time of the Judges (see Ruth 1:1); it forms a link between the days when "there was no king in Israel" (Judges 21:25) and the time of King David, who sat on "the throne of the LORD", in Jerusalem.

The story starts in Moab: Naomi and her husband Elimelech had moved there, seeking relief from the famine in Judea. Elimelech died in Moab; their two sons also died, leaving Naomi with her daughters-in-law, Orpah and Ruth. Orpah chose to stay in Moab, but—when the famine was over—Ruth accompanied Naomi back to Judea. Ruth the Moabitess learned from Naomi about the God of Israel, in whom she came to trust (2:12). In Bethlehem, Naomi's home town, an elderly relation, Boaz, showed kindness to them both. Eventually he married Ruth and the happy result was the birth of a son, Obed, who was the grandfather of King David. Some 1,000 years later, Mary the mother of Jesus was born of this family line (see family tree).

God's Harvest

Ruth came to Bethlehem (the 'house of bread'!) at the time of barley harvest. At first she was allowed to glean corn dropped in the field which belonged to Boaz. Later she was invited to share the meals he provided for his servants.

God is preparing a people for His coming Kingdom, where believers from all down the ages will eat and drink with Jesus, the first-fruits of that final harvest! (Luke 22:30; 1 Corinthians 15:23).

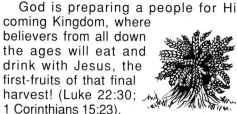

Some interesting links with other parts of the Bible

For example:

a) Ruth 1:6
b) Ruth 2:12
c) Ruth 4:17-22

Compared with:

a) Exodus 4:31; Luke 1:68
b) Psalm 17:8; Matthew 23:37
c) Matthew 1:3-6; Luke 1:30-32; 3:31-33

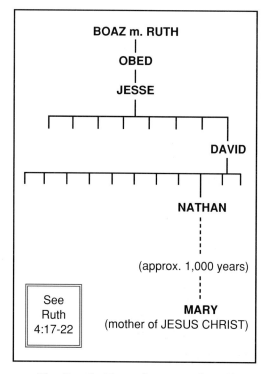

BOAZ m. RUTH

OBED

JESSE

DAVID

NATHAN

(approx. 1,000 years)

See Ruth 4:17-22

MARY (mother of JESUS CHRIST)

The Family Tree of Boaz and Ruth

1 SAMUEL

Events at the time of Samuel the prophet: the reign of King Saul over Israel; God's choice of David to be the King of His people, instead of Saul.

David and Goliath

In the days of Eli, Hannah—a Godly but childless woman—prays for a son. Samuel is born and she devotes him to the Lord's service. Samuel's life is then spent restoring Israel's worship—and being a Kingmaker.

Perhaps the best known event in this book is in ch 17. With a single stone from his sling, David the shepherd-boy defeated the great Philistine champion, Goliath. This showed God was on David's side.

Jesus and the Gentiles

This incident is a remarkable foretaste of how Jesus (the "Son of David") will overthrow the kingdoms of men and all Gentile domination, when he returns to re-establish God's Kingdom in Israel (compare the prophecy of Daniel 2).

Samuel the Prophet (40 years)

• The ark (from the Tabernacle) was captured by the Philistines (ch 4) but later returned (ch 5).

• Israel asked for a king (ch 8), though their God was their King!

• Samuel was told by God to anoint Saul as king (ch 9).

King Saul (40 years)

• Saul disobeyed God (chs 13 & 15), so God rejected him and told Samuel to anoint David, "a man after God's own heart".

• Saul envied David and often tried to kill him (chs 18-31).

King David (40 years)

• After the death of Saul, David became king, first in Hebron (7 years), then in Jerusalem (33 years). (The record continues into 2 Samuel.)

Some interesting links with other parts of the Bible

For example:	Compared with:
a) 1 Samuel 15:22	a) Micah 6:6-8
b) 1 Samuel 17:49	b) Daniel 2:34,44,45
c) 1 Samuel 18:5, 14,30	c) Luke 2:52

"The LORD seeth not as man seeth; for man looketh on the outward appearance, but the LORD looketh on the heart"
(16:7)

10 2 SAMUEL

The reign of King David over God's Kingdom in Israel. Jerusalem is made capital city. David's sin and the troubles which followed.

Two Main Sections

This Book has two parts, covering the period when David was King:

First, after the death of King Saul, David became King in Hebron (7 years) and later in Jerusalem (33 years). With God's help, surrounding enemy nations were subdued. David brought back the ark of God up to Jerusalem (ch 6).

David had built himself a house of cedar-wood, and wanted to provide a more permanent resting-place for the ark of God—a centre for Israel's worship to take the place of the Tabernacle in the wilderness. Through the prophet Nathan, God told David that "thy seed after thee …

shall build an house for my name" (7:12,13): that was to be Solomon. But the prophecy was not limited to Solomon. God promised David that, although he would not have the privilege of building God's house, "the LORD will make *thee* an house"; moreover, speaking of his "seed" (offspring or descendant), "I will establish the throne of his kingdom for ever" (7:11-13). This greater "Son of David" is Jesus Christ (see Luke 1:32,33; 18:38).

David's Sin

The second section begins in ch 11 with David's great sin in taking Bathsheba, the wife of Uriah. Bathsheba bore a baby son, who in spite of David's prayers, died; but then Bathsheba bore Solomon, who was to succeed David.

Although David repented of his sin (see his plea for God's mercy and lovingkindness in Psalm 51), and God forgave him, he suffered thereafter at the hands of his own family. His son Absalom rebelled, taking the throne temporarily, and David had to flee. Later he was able to return to Jerusalem. Chs 22-23 contain prophecies of Christ's future reign.

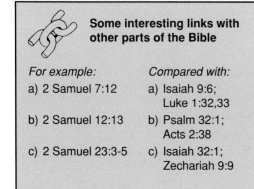

Some interesting links with other parts of the Bible

For example:
a) 2 Samuel 7:12
b) 2 Samuel 12:13
c) 2 Samuel 23:3-5

Compared with:
a) Isaiah 9:6; Luke 1:32,33
b) Psalm 32:1; Acts 2:38
c) Isaiah 32:1; Zechariah 9:9

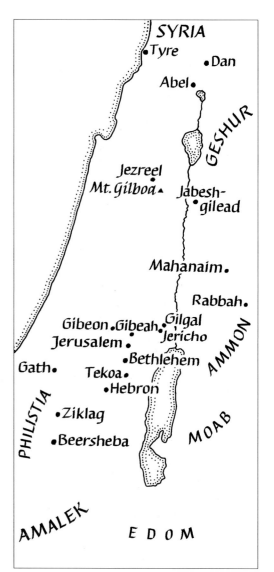

Places named in 2 Samuel

1 KINGS

The reign of King Solomon (40 years) and the first 85 years of the divided Kingdom. The spread of idolatry in the North, in spite of the work of the prophet Elijah.

The Kingdom of God

The two Books of Kings record the history of the 'Kingdom of God' in the past with its capital, Jerusalem. King David (ch 1) and Solomon (chs 2-11) ruled a united kingdom, but decay set in following Solomon's turning to idolatry (ch 11).

The kingdom was divided in the reign of Solomon's son, Rehoboam. Various wicked kings ruled the Northern section, whilst descendants of David continued to rule in Jerusalem.

The Temple of God

The temple built by Solomon (chs 5-8) was similar in design to the Tabernacle, though the sizes of the two main rooms were doubled and the number of lampstands and washing places (lavers) were now ten.

Built in a time of peace, this temple pointed forward to a future one, when the Kingdom of God will be restored in Israel —at a time of peace, with Jesus Christ as King! (Zechariah 6:13).

King Solomon

This great monarch was famed for his wisdom and wealth. The Queen of Sheba (southern Arabia) paid a state visit (ch 10). Solomon's ships brought gold from afar.

Elijah the Prophet

Elijah (chs 17-22) was a prophet of God to the Northern Kingdom (Israel). He showed who was the true God when, on Mt. Carmel, and in the sight of all the false prophets, he called on God to send down fire from heaven.

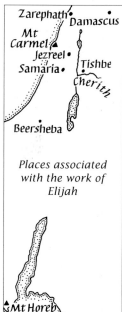

Places associated with the work of Elijah

Some interesting links with other parts of the Bible

For example:
a) 1 Kings 13:18
b) 1 Kings 18:21
c) 1 Kings 22:24

Compared with:
a) Galatians 1:8
b) Isaiah 44:6; John 17:3
c) Micah 5:1; Matthew 26:67

'Ships of Tarshish' (1 Kings 10:22)

(Temple diagram labels: Lavers, MOST HOLY PLACE, ark, incense altar, HOLY PLACE, lamp-stands, PORCH)

2 KINGS

A record of the divided Kingdom until the overthrow of Israel by Assyria in 722 BC and of Judah 136 years later, by Babylon.

Two Kingdoms Topple

Disobedience of God's Word, and idolatry in the Northern Kingdom of Israel, resulted in the downfall of that kingdom in 722 BC.

The Southern Kingdom of Judah, which had a few better kings (shown by an asterisk on the chart) was finally overthrown by Nebuchadnezzar, King of Babylon, in 586 BC. Many of the Jews were taken into captivity in Babylon.

The Prophet Elisha

After he had seen Elijah taken away (ch 2), Elisha became the next great prophet to Israel. He asked Elijah for "a double portion of thy spirit" (v 9), and the number and nature of the miracles Elisha performed—e.g. healing the waters of a spring (2 Kings 2:19), increasing the widow's oil (4:1), bringing the Shunammite's son back to life (4:34), causing an axe-head to float to the surface (6:1) etc.—suggest that God granted the request. One miracle with a specially significant spiritual lesson was the cleansing from leprosy of Naaman, the Syrian commander-in-chief (ch 5). By humbling himself and being willing to wash in the waters of the river Jordan, Naaman prefigured the act of baptism which Jesus commanded, which can cleanse a sinner and give him or her a new life: a 'burial' in water followed by a 'resurrection' to a new way of life.

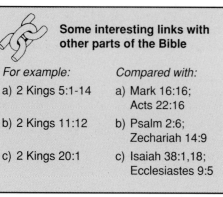

Some interesting links with other parts of the Bible

For example:

a) 2 Kings 5:1-14

b) 2 Kings 11:12

c) 2 Kings 20:1

Compared with:

a) Mark 16:16;
   Acts 22:16

b) Psalm 2:6;
   Zechariah 14:9

c) Isaiah 38:1,18;
   Ecclesiastes 9:5

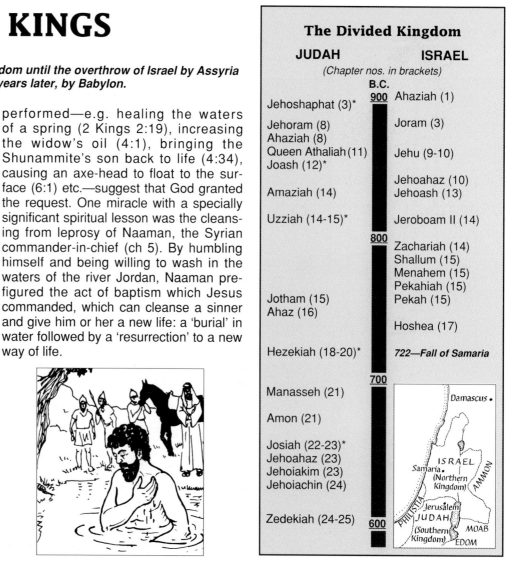

The Divided Kingdom

JUDAH	ISRAEL
(Chapter nos. in brackets)	
B.C.	
Jehoshaphat (3)* — **900**	Ahaziah (1)
Jehoram (8)	Joram (3)
Ahaziah (8)	
Queen Athaliah (11)	
Joash (12)*	Jehu (9-10)
	Jehoahaz (10)
Amaziah (14)	Jehoash (13)
Uzziah (14-15)*	Jeroboam II (14)
800	
	Zachariah (14)
	Shallum (15)
	Menahem (15)
	Pekahiah (15)
Jotham (15)	Pekah (15)
Ahaz (16)	
	Hoshea (17)
Hezekiah (18-20)*	*722—Fall of Samaria*
700	
Manasseh (21)	
Amon (21)	
Josiah (22-23)*	
Jehoahaz (23)	
Jehoiakim (23)	
Jehoiachin (24)	
Zedekiah (24-25) — **600**	

1 CHRONICLES

13

God's dealings with Judah in the days of David; the "mighty men", the priesthood and servants involved in the praise and worship of God during David's reign and in preparation for Solomon's reign.

The wings of the cherubim in the Most Holy Place were fully outstretched— symbolic of the world-wide worship of the future age (2 Chronicles 3:11-13; Zechariah 14:9)

Cymbals (see 16:5)

A silver trumpet as used by the priests (see 15:24; 16:6)

Jerusalem Journals

The Hebrew name for the two Books of Chronicles means 'the Acts of the Days'. In the Septuagint, the Chronicles are referred to by a Greek word which means 'the things omitted'—suggesting that it was viewed as a supplement to the other historical writings. They are journals or records of events in God's ancient Kingdom centred in Jerusalem, when David and subsequent kings sat on "the throne of the Lord".

1 Chronicles commences with several chapters of genealogies—reminding God's people of their ancestry and heritage, and particularly of their function as witnesses to God among the nations. Later chapters cover the same ground as the end of 1 Samuel, much of 2 Samuel and the start of 1 Kings; but this book emphasies spiritual themes. There is much in these divinely inspired books which looks forward to the restoration of God's Kingdom in Israel, under Jesus Christ. Even now, true servants of God can learn how to worship in the "beauty of holiness" (or 'holy attire'), being clad with the "righteousness of Christ" through belief, baptism and obedience (see Galatians 3:27; Ephesians 4:24).

Preparations for the Temple

David himself was not allowed to build a temple for God: "God said unto me, Thou shalt not build a house for my name, because thou hast been a man of war" (28:3). David did, however, prepare the materials needed to build the temple, and prayed that God would "give unto Solomon my son a perfect heart, to keep thy commandments ... and to build the palace (temple), for the which I have made provision" (29:19).

So David died, "full of days, riches, and honour: and Solomon his son reigned in his stead" (29:28).

Some interesting links with other parts of the Bible

For example:	Compared with:
a) 1 Chronicles 16:29	a) Psalm 96:9-10; Psalm 110:3
b) 1 Chronicles 17:11-14	b) Isaiah 9:6,7; Luke 1:32-33
c) 1 Chronicles 28:5; 29:23	c) 2 Chronicles 13:8; Acts 1:6

2 CHRONICLES

The reigns of Solomon, and of the later kings in Judah, emphasise the blessings received when the Jews gave glory to God and were faithful.

The Nation Needs God

The Second Book of Chronicles, which parallels much of 1 & 2 Kings, continues the theme of the First Book, showing how the Jews found their greatest blessings when they worshipped God truly and tried to obey His laws.

Instances are highlighted in which the religious zeal of the king, or the people, resulted in victories and in a period of peace, whereas wickedness led only to defeat and trouble. By such means God sought to teach His nation (see, for example, 20:22; 26:5; 30:9).

The Temple

The early chapters provide details of the small but perfect Temple, built to Divine plans, which was erected in the reign of Solomon and lasted 430 years—the period covered by 2 Chronicles.

When it was first built, the Temple was temporarily filled with the "glory of God" (7:1-3). This remarkable event pointed forward to the future Kingdom of God, when his "glory" will fill the whole earth (Numbers 14:21). When there is "glory to God" then, too, there will be "peace on earth" (Luke 2:14).

Solomon's Temple

"Blessed be the LORD thy God, which delighted in thee, to set thee on his throne, to be king for the LORD thy God" (words of the Queen of Sheba to Solomon, 9:8)

Some interesting links with other parts of the Bible

For example:
a) 2 Chronicles 7:1-2
b) 2 Chronicles 20:17
c) 2 Chronicles 36:16

Compared with:
a) Ezekiel 43:4,5; Isaiah 11:9
b) Exodus 14:13; Psalm 46:10
c) Jeremiah 25:3,4; Matthew 23:34-39

King	Years	Type	See 2 Chronicles
Rehoboam	17	Bad	12:1-2
Abijah	3	GOOD	13:10-12
Asa	41	GOOD	15:15-17
Jehoshaphat	25	GOOD	17:3-6
Jehoram	8	Bad	21:12-15
Ahaziah	1	Bad	22:2-7
Q. Athaliah	6	Bad	23:12-15
Joash	40	GOOD	24:8-10
Amaziah	29	Bad	25:14-16
Uzziah	52	GOOD	26:3-15
Jotham	16	Bad	27:2-6
Ahaz	16	Bad	28:1-5
Hezekiah	29	GOOD	31:20-21
Manasseh	55	Bad	33:9-11
Amon	2	Bad	33:21-24
Josiah	31	GOOD	34:1-7
Jehoahaz	3m	Bad	36:1-3
Jehoiakim	11	Bad	36:5-6
Jehoiachin	3m	Bad	36:9-10
Zedekiah	11	Bad	36:11-17

EZRA

The Cylinder of Cyrus

The return of the Jews from captivity in Babylon, led first by Zerubbabel and Joshua and later by Ezra the Scribe. The Temple was rebuilt in spite of opposition from adversaries living in the land.

15

Kings of the Medes and Persians	
B.C.	
540 Cyrus (1:1)	*Zerubbabel and Joshua*
530 Cambyses (4:6) Smerdis (4:7)	
520 Darius I (4:24)	*Haggai and Zechariah*
510	
500	
490 Xerxes I	
480 (Esther 1:1)	
470 Artaxerxes I (7:1)	
460	*Ezra*
450	
440	*Nehemiah*

The Cylinder of Cyrus

The Persian monarch, Cyrus I, recorded his exploits on a clay cylinder, now in the British Museum. The inscriptions on it include his decree made in 536 BC, which allowed the Jews who were in exile in Babylonia and Persia to return to Israel.

This fulfilled God's promise, made through the prophet Jeremiah, that the Jews would be able to come back from Babylon after 70 years of captivity (see Jeremiah 29:10).

Enemies of Israel

A small number of Jews returned under the initial decree of Cyrus (ch 2). These were led by Zerubbabel (a prince of the royal tribe of Judah) and Joshua (the High Priest).

Adversaries interfered with the rebuilding of the Temple (ch 4) having cunningly obtained a decree from the new Persian king, Smerdis ('Artaxerxes', ch 4:7), forbidding the Jewish activities.

However, God's prophets Haggai and Zechariah encouraged the Jews to resume the work, and the next Persian king, Darius I, supported them (chs 5-6).

Ezra the Scribe

Ezra, a priest and scribe of the Law, led a second wave of Jews, about 70 years after the initial return. From ch 7 onwards, we learn of this and of Ezra's efforts to reform the nation. He taught them the Word of God and showed them their need for total separation from the false worship and ways of the nations round about them. In ch 9 is recorded his moving prayer of repentance on behalf of the people: "And now, O our God, what shall we say after this? for we have forsaken thy commandments ... Thou hast punished us less than our iniquities deserve" (9:10-13).

	Some interesting links with other parts of the Bible

For example:	*Compared with:*
a) Ezra 5:1,2	a) Haggai 1:1; Zechariah 1:1
b) Ezra 5:5	b) Psalm 33:18; 34:15; 1 Peter 3:12
c) Ezra 9:14	c) 2 Corinthians 6:17; Revelation 18:4

16

NEHEMIAH

Nehemiah, a Jewish cup bearer to the King of Persia, becomes Governor in Jerusalem and encourages the rebuilding of the city walls, in the face of opposition.

The Cup Bearer

Nehemiah was a Jewish exile who served as a cup bearer to the Persian monarch, Artaxerxes, about 446 BC. Following the decree of Cyrus in 536 BC some of the Jews had returned to the land of Israel. However, adversaries had succeeded in slowing down the work of restoration. Now, some 90 years later, the walls of Jerusalem were in a state of disrepair. Nehemiah prayed to God about it (1:4).

Sorrow for Jerusalem

Nehemiah's sorrow for the state of Jerusalem showed in his face. Artaxerxes demanded to know the reason for Nehemiah's fallen countenance. A quick prayer to God by Nehemiah (2:4) was immediately answered. Artaxerxes gave Nehemiah authority to go to Jerusalem and personally take charge of the rebuilding work.

The wall is finished

Despite further opposition from "Arabians, Ammonites and Ashdodites", and others, the wall was completed in a mere 52 days (6:15)!

Ezra the scribe had returned to Jerusalem some 11 years earlier (Ezra 7)

and for a while had been able to instruct and encourage the Jews in the ways of God. Now, with Nehemiah as Governor of the Land, opposition was kept at bay, though the Jews themselves needed further reform.

The Reading of God's Word

The people were helped most when Ezra and his assistant priests read daily to them from God's Word, when they assembled with their families in the streets of Jerusalem. They saw the need to change their ways. All were in need, including some religious leaders—who were among the worst offenders (13:29).

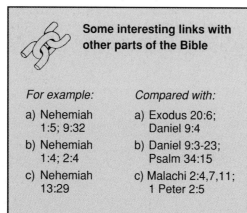

Some interesting links with other parts of the Bible

For example:

a) Nehemiah 1:5; 9:32

b) Nehemiah 1:4; 2:4

c) Nehemiah 13:29

Compared with:

a) Exodus 20:6; Daniel 9:4

b) Daniel 9:3-23; Psalm 34:15

c) Malachi 2:4,7,11; 1 Peter 2:5

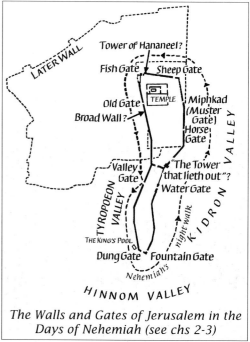

The Walls and Gates of Jerusalem in the Days of Nehemiah (see chs 2-3)

ESTHER

A Divine Record of an attempted massacre of the Jews throughout the Persian Empire. The providential intervention of Esther, a Jewess.

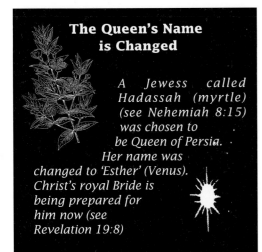

The Queen's Name is Changed

A Jewess called Hadassah (myrtle) (see Nehemiah 8:15) was chosen to be Queen of Persia. Her name was changed to 'Esther' (Venus). Christ's royal Bride is being prepared for him now (see Revelation 19:8)

The World Empire of Persia

The Persian Empire spread over much of the civilised world and consisted of 127 provinces from India to Ethiopia (1:1). Many Jews were still scattered throughout the Empire (4:3; 8:9,17) during the time of Esther and King Xerxes (485-464 BC).

An attempt to annihilate the Jews was thwarted by God, who has an on-going purpose with this nation.

The Conquest of the Enemy

There are three main sections:

King Ahasuerus (Xerxes) rejected Queen Vashti and chose a new queen, whom he named Esther. She had been brought up by Mordecai, her cousin, who was also Jewish. Haman was a wicked Amalekite, of a tribe long opposed to Israel and to God (see Exodus 17:8-16; Numbers 24:20). He was jealous of Mordecai and planned to destroy him and all Jews on a date decided by casting 'lots' (Purim) (3:7,13).

Mordecai persuaded Esther to plead with the King for her people. So she began by inviting the King and Haman to a banquet. At a second banquet she told the King of Haman's plot to massacre the Jews. The King commanded that Haman should be hung on the 50 cubits (75 ft) high 'tree' which Haman had prepared for the hanging of Mordecai (5:14; 7:10).

The King then issued a decree permitting all Jews to defend themselves on the appointed day. This deliverance is commemorated by the Jews every year at the Feast of Purim (9:27,28).

Jesus Conquered Sin

Jesus, too, was hung on a 'tree' (Acts 5:30). He did so as a representative of sinful mankind. But God raised him from the dead, so giving hope to those who believe and follow him (Romans 6:4,22).

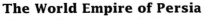

Some interesting links with other parts of the Bible

For example:	Compared with:
a) Esther 2:12,17	a) Revelation 19:7,8; Psalm 45:10-17
b) Esther 5:14; 7:10	b) Acts 5:30; 10:39; Galatians 3:13; 1 Peter 2:24
c) Esther 10:3	c) Genesis 41:40,43; Matthew 27:29; 28:18

Time Chart: Old Testament Events

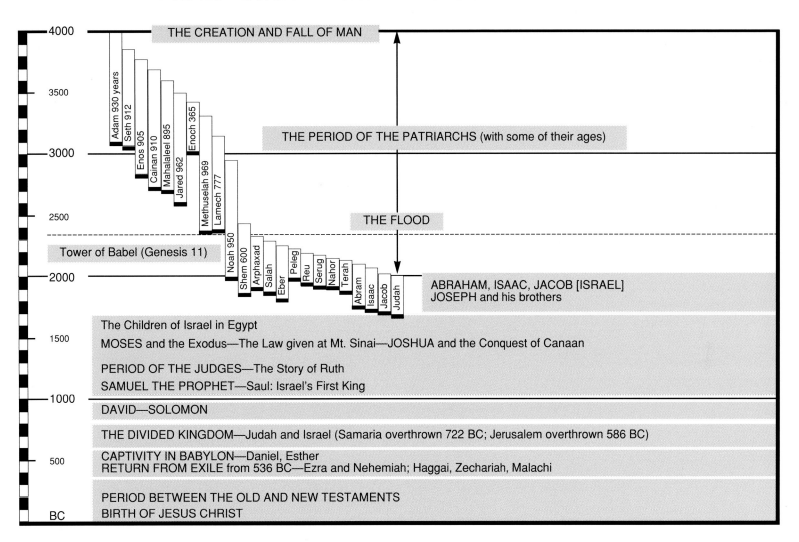

THE CREATION AND FALL OF MAN

Adam 930 years
Seth 912
Enos 905
Cainan 910
Mahalaleel 895
Jared 962
Enoch 365
Methuselah 969
Lamech 777

THE PERIOD OF THE PATRIARCHS (with some of their ages)

THE FLOOD

Tower of Babel (Genesis 11)

Noah 950
Shem 600
Arphaxad
Salah
Eber
Peleg
Reu
Serug
Nahor
Terah
Abram
Isaac
Jacob
Judah

ABRAHAM, ISAAC, JACOB [ISRAEL]
JOSEPH and his brothers

The Children of Israel in Egypt

MOSES and the Exodus—The Law given at Mt. Sinai—JOSHUA and the Conquest of Canaan

PERIOD OF THE JUDGES—The Story of Ruth

SAMUEL THE PROPHET—Saul: Israel's First King

DAVID—SOLOMON

THE DIVIDED KINGDOM—Judah and Israel (Samaria overthrown 722 BC; Jerusalem overthrown 586 BC)

CAPTIVITY IN BABYLON—Daniel, Esther
RETURN FROM EXILE from 536 BC—Ezra and Nehemiah; Haggai, Zechariah, Malachi

PERIOD BETWEEN THE OLD AND NEW TESTAMENTS
BIRTH OF JESUS CHRIST

4000
3500
3000
2500
2000
1500
1000
500
BC

Family Tree: From Adam to Jesus Christ

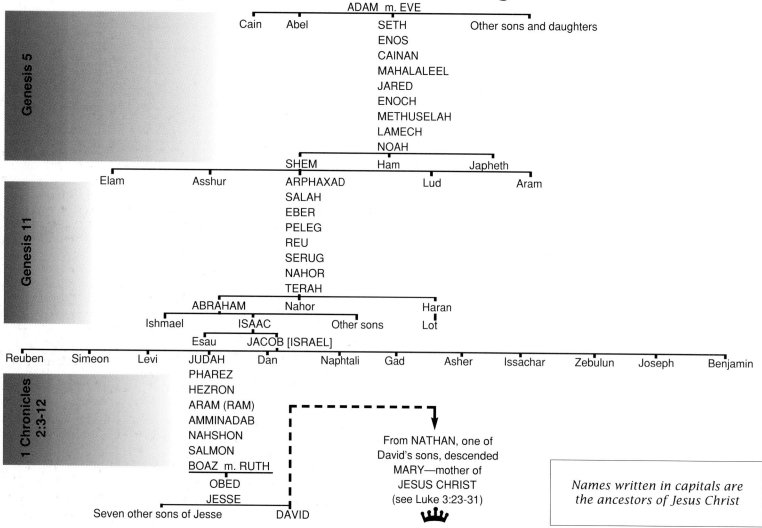

ADAM m. EVE

| Genesis 5 | Cain | Abel | SETH | Other sons and daughters |

SETH
ENOS
CAINAN
MAHALALEEL
JARED
ENOCH
METHUSELAH
LAMECH
NOAH

SHEM Ham Japheth

Genesis 11

Elam Asshur ARPHAXAD Lud Aram
SALAH
EBER
PELEG
REU
SERUG
NAHOR
TERAH

ABRAHAM Nahor Haran
Ishmael ISAAC Other sons Lot
Esau JACOB [ISRAEL]

Reuben Simeon Levi JUDAH Dan Naphtali Gad Asher Issachar Zebulun Joseph Benjamin

1 Chronicles 2:3-12

PHAREZ
HEZRON
ARAM (RAM)
AMMINADAB
NAHSHON
SALMON
BOAZ m. RUTH
OBED
JESSE

Seven other sons of Jesse DAVID

From NATHAN, one of
David's sons, descended
MARY—mother of
JESUS CHRIST
(see Luke 3:23-31)

*Names written in capitals are
the ancestors of Jesus Christ*

POETRY SECTION

"Praise ye the LORD.
Sing unto the LORD a new song,
And his praise in the assembly of the saints."

(Psalm 149:1)

Books 18-22

Introduction to the
POETRY SECTION

Chapters in the Poetic Books

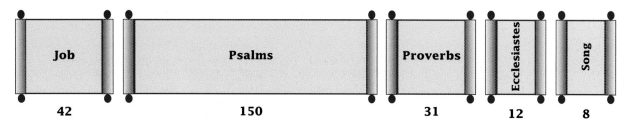

Job	Psalms	Proverbs	Ecclesiastes	Song
42	150	31	12	8

The Nature of Hebrew Poetry

Hebrew poetry differs from prose mainly in the rhythmic style in which it is written. Its purpose is usually to provide praise, prayer or instruction which can be sung, or accompanied by music.

Thus lines are repeated, or the ideas put another way, or the opposite is expressed, so as to serve as responses. Clear examples are to be found in the Psalms in which two groups of singers would be intended—as in Psalm 24:8:

Question put by first group: "Who is this King of Glory?"
Reply by second group: "The LORD strong and mighty"

Teaching through Poetry

One of the most important uses to which this poetic style is put in God's Books is to impress on us important attitudes of mind. Sometimes by repetition, sometimes by contrast (as in Proverbs) God seeks to underline both His message and what our response to it should be. The Lord Jesus Christ read the Poetic Books, as well as all the other Old Testament Scriptures, and saw how he could apply them to his own experience.

A helpful Christadelphian book which deals with the subject of poetry and music in the Bible is
Exploring the Psalms by Mark Vincent

JOB

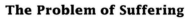

The story of the sufferings of Job and the attempted explanation of these events by his friends. God's own answer is given.

18

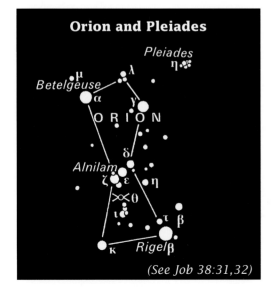

Orion and Pleiades

Pleiades

Betelgeuse

O R I O N

Alnilam

Rigel

(See Job 38:31,32)

The Problem of Suffering

The setting of the book is the "land of Uz", probably Edom, at the time of the patriarchs. The theme is the age-old 'problem of suffering'. God allowed intense suffering to afflict Job—a "good" man who was well respected by all. But Job's friends—Eliphaz, Bildad and Zophar—wrongly assumed that his sufferings were punishments for hidden sins. "Miserable comforters are ye all" (16:2) is Job's assessment of his friends!

A fourth 'friend', the younger man Elihu, is introduced in ch 32. He was angry with Job, "because he justified himself rather than God" and against the three friends "because they had found no answer, and yet had condemned Job."

God's Answer

But finally, in chs 38-41, we read God's answer to the matter. He reminds Job of his true position before God the Creator. Job was brought to realise that God is right and should be trusted. Job confesses his own unworthiness (even though people had looked upon him as good). His sufferings helped him to see this point, and he was eventually richly blessed (42:10).

If suffering brings us to a position of humility before God, it will prove to be blessing in disguise (see Isaiah 66:2).

Job's Satan

The story of Job refers to a "satan" (a word meaning 'adversary'). The Bible never speaks of a supernatural Devil. Job's "satan" was someone to whom God temporarily gave the power to bring certain troubles upon Job for his good—see Job 2:6 and 42:11; in fact, the second of these verses refers to "all the evil that the LORD had brought upon him".

God, in the end, restores the fortunes of Job and requires the three friends to offer sacrifices, "for ye have not spoken of me the thing that is right, as my servant Job hath" (42:7).

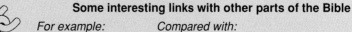

Some interesting links with other parts of the Bible	
For example:	*Compared with:*
a) Job 4:17; 14:10	a) Psalm 146:3-4; Ecclesiastes 9:5; Romans 5:12
b) Job 19:25	b) Zechariah 14:4; Acts 1:11
c) Job 38:31-41	c) Amos 5:8; Acts 14:15; Revelation 14:7

PSALMS

Songs of Praise, Prayer and Prophecy, written by David, Hezekiah and others. Many are about the promised Messiah, pointing forward to his suffering, resurrection and future rule.

"I have set the LORD always before me: because he is at my right hand, I shall not be moved." (16:8)

Five Main Sections

There are five books of Psalms. Each ends with words of praise or a final "Amen".

1-41	PSALMS OF DAVID
42-72	PSALMS OF DAVID AND OF THE SONS OF KORAH
73-89	PSALMS OF ASAPH AND OTHERS
90-106	PSALMS OF MOSES AND OTHERS
107-150	PSALMS OF DAVID, HEZEKIAH, ETC.

The Psalms and Music

The Psalms were originally sung, and accompanied by musical instruments (a number of Psalms have instructions to the musicians in their 'titles'). They were intended for personal use as well as for congregational worship.

Christ in the Psalms

The work of Christ was foretold in the Psalms and indeed in all parts of the Old Testament (see Luke 24:44). Jesus knew the Psalms. In effect, they became his words.

Some Psalms are obviously about him:
- CHRIST'S SUFFERINGS—
  Psalms 22; 40; 109; 118
- HIS RESURRECTION—
  Psalms 16; 91
- HIS FUTURE RULE—
  Psalms 2; 24; 45; 72; 110; 122

Personal Treasure

Over the centuries faithful men and women have derived great personal strength and comfort from the Psalms. There are chapters suited to almost every occasion for the true believer—times of sorrow, danger or joy.

Psalm 119 has 22 sections, in each of which the verses begin with the same letter of the Hebrew alphabet. But the Psalm is particularly notable as *every* verse refers either to God's Word, or to His laws, commandments, precepts, statutes, testimonies, and judgements.

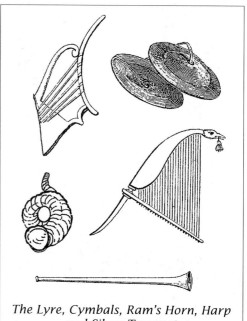

The Lyre, Cymbals, Ram's Horn, Harp and Silver Trumpet

Some interesting links with other parts of the Bible

For example:	Compared with:
a) Psalm 2:8,9	a) Revelation 2:26,27
b Psalm 16:10	b) Acts 2:27, 31
c) Psalm 72:8	c) Zechariah 9:10

PROVERBS

20

Wise sayings, written mainly by King Solomon, under the inspiration of God. They contain sound advice for all God's children.

"Have not I written to thee excellent things in counsel and knowledge ... That I might make thee know the certainty of the words of truth ... "

Proverbs 22:20,21

"Go to the ant thou sluggard ... Consider her ways and be wise ... " (6:6)

Solomon's Request

God appeared to King Solomon and said, "Ask what I shall give thee." Solomon might have desired wealth and power, but he made a surprising request: "Give me now wisdom and knowledge ... for who can judge this thy people, that is so great?" (2 Chronicles 1:7-10). "And all the kings of the earth sought the presence of Solomon, to hear his wisdom, that God had put in his heart" (9:23).

The Value of Wisdom

The opening chapters are addressed to "my son" (chs 1-9). Sadly, Solomon's son (Rehoboam) failed to heed the Divine instruction.

It was God's Son, the Lord Jesus Christ, who recognised the value of his Father's Word.

For us, too, there is nothing in this world which can compare with this "wisdom which is from above", to be found in the Bible—in all God's 66 Books, including this Book of Proverbs.

Advice for Daily Life

A large section of Proverbs (chs 10-24) contains valuable advice for God's children in their day to day experiences. The ruin which comes from sloth and the folly of ignorance are among the warnings given.

Chs 25-29 contain more proverbs of Solomon, copied out by King Hezekiah's men. The writers of Proverbs 30-31 may have been Arabian, descended from Ishmael; or "Agur" and "Lemuel" may be cryptic names for Solomon himself.

"And he (Solomon) spake three thousand proverbs: and his songs were a thousand and five."

(1 Kings 4:32)

Some interesting links with other parts of the Bible

For example:
a) Proverbs 3:15; 4:7
b) Proverbs 7:19,20

c) Proverbs 22:20,21

Compared with:
a) 2 Timothy 3:15
b) Mark 13:34; Luke 12:45

c) Luke 1:3,4

21 ECCLESIASTES

The vanity of life apart from God. Solomon shows that to fear God and keep His commandments is the only thing that really matters.

The alternative title of this Book is "The Preacher", and the opening verse identifies the writer as "the Preacher, the son of David, king in Jerusalem".

"All go unto one place"

King Solomon's riches, wisdom and exploits were proverbial. Yet in this Book, the vanity of all life apart from God is underlined. Without His Word, and our response to it, all would be pointless. We would all end up, like animals, in the dust of death; for in the grave all life and consciousness ceases (Ecclesiastes 3:19,20; 9:4-6). This is the consistent teaching of all Scripture, but in Ecclesiastes it is repeated time after time, unmistakably.

"Remember now thy Creator"

Old age brings its problems, as the various parts of the body are affected. Different parts of the body, as well as various senses, may be referred to in the poetic language of ch 12 (see table). The Divine advice is to remember our Creator while we have life, vigour and opportunity (see 12:1).

The Only True Hope

The whole purpose of life is to glorify God (12:13). There is a day of judgement to come (v 14). In other parts of His Word, God offers us hope of eternal life in an eternal body, following resurrection and judgement at the return of Christ. This will enable us to live for ever on a renewed and perfect planet Earth.

This great promise rests on our belief and obedience *now* !

Some interesting links with other parts of the Bible

For example:
a) Ecclesiastes 3:20
b) Ecclesiastes 7:20
c) Ecclesiastes 12:8

Compared with:
a) Genesis 3:19; Romans 5:12
b) Romans 3:23; 1 John 1:8
c) Psalm 62:9; 1 Corinthians 15:14,58

A Picture of Mortal Man (ch 12)

"Keepers of the house tremble"	*Arms*
"Strong men shall bow themselves"	*Legs*
"The grinders cease"	*Teeth*
"Those that look out of the windows"	*Eyes*
"Doors shall be shut"	*Mouth?*
"Rise up at the voice of a bird"	*Light sleeper*
"Daughters of music brought low"	*Deafness sets in*
"Afraid of that which is high"	*Fear of heights*
"The almond tree shall blossom"	*White hair?*
"The grasshopper shall drag itself along" (RV margin)	*The burden of age*
"Desire (RV caperberry—a condiment) shall fail"	*Taste fades*
"The silver cord ... the golden bowl broken"	*Lamp of life extinguished*
"Pitcher broken at the fountain ... wheel broken at the cistern"	*Life (the supply of the water of life) fails*
"Dust returns to the earth"	*Death*

SONG OF SOLOMON

22

This Book from God depicts His love for Israel, and looks ahead to the love of Christ for his Bride, to be fully realised when he returns to earth.

The Turtle Dove

God's Love for Israel

This "Song of Songs" (see 1:1) has for its theme the quality of Divine love. This is illustrated in God's love for His people, whom he describes elsewhere as his "Bride" (see, for example, Isaiah 54:5,6).

Christ's Love for his Bride

The story is woven around the Shulamite, the shepherd and the king; but also involves groups of women, watchmen and other characters.

The love of the bridegroom for his bride, and her response, is beautifully portrayed in this tender allegory, pointing forward to the love of Christ for his true followers, and their devotion to him. The intimate relationship which will exist between them is likened in the Song to that between the dove and its mate, which is a lifelong partnership (2:14).

The Marriage Feast

The return of the Bridegroom (i.e. the return of Christ) will be followed by the perfecting of the Bride, when faithful followers of Christ will be made both sinless and immortal.

Thus the words of 4:7 will be made true: "You are all fair, my love; there is no flaw in you". The "marriage of the Lamb" to his Bride can take place, as foretold in Revelation 19:6-8. This means they will be united, both in immortality and in outlook, with Christ and also with God Himself (see John 17:21).

The Inheritance

Together, the Bridegroom and the Bride will inherit the Promised Land: this will extend to the whole Earth. Paradise will be restored and all creation will rejoice.

Some interesting links with other parts of the Bible

For example:	*Compared with:*
a) Song 1:3,12	a) John 12:3
b) Song 4:7	b) Ephesians 5:25-27
c) Song 5:16	c) Psalm 45:11; Isaiah 33:17; John 1:14

PROPHECY SECTION

"Surely the Lord GOD will do nothing,
but he revealeth his secret unto his servants
the prophets." *(Amos 3:7)*

Books 23-39

Time Chart of the Kings and Prophets

Prophets	Kings (and Leaders)		Other Empires and Kings
The prophets who wrote books are in bold type	David *(who replaced Saul)* Solomon		
	Israel	**Judah**	
	Jeroboam I Nadab Baasha … Omri	Rehoboam Abijah Asa	
Elijah Elisha	Ahab Ahaziah Joram Jehu Jehoahaz Jehoash	Jehoshaphat Jehoram Ahaziah Q. Athaliah Joash Amaziah	**Assyria** Shalmaneser III
Joel **Jonah** **Amos** **Hosea** **Micah** **Isaiah**	Jeroboam II Zechariah, Shallum Menahem Pekahiah Pekah Hoshea	Uzziah (Azariah) Jotham Ahaz Hezekiah	Tiglath-pileser III Shalmaneser V Sargon Sennacherib
Nahum **Zephaniah** **Jeremiah** **Habakkuk**	Fall of Samaria 722 BC	Manasseh Amon Josiah Jehoahaz, Jehoiakim, Jehoiachin, Zedekiah	Esarhaddon Ashurbanipal **Babylon**
Obadiah **Daniel** **Ezekiel**		Fall of Jerusalem 586 BC	Nebuchadnezzar Nabonidus Belshazzar **Persia**
Haggai		(Zerubbabel)	Cyrus Darius
Zechariah **Malachi**		 (Ezra) (Nehemiah)	Xerxes I (Ahasuerus) Artaxerxes I

Timeline (BC): 1000, 900, 800, 700, 600, 500, 400

70 years captivity in Babylon (586-516 BC)

Decree of Cyrus, allowing return, 536 BC

"He was despised and rejected of men; a man of sorrows and acquainted with grief ... All we like sheep have gone astray; we have turned every one to his own way; and the LORD hath laid on him the iniquity of us all" (53:3-6)

ISAIAH

23

In this lovely Book, we learn of the holiness of God and of His promise of a Saviour and King for all nations in the future age when Jerusalem will be His capital city.

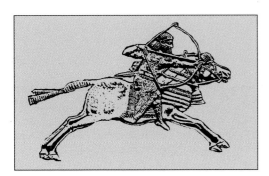

Ashurbanipal the Assyrian

A clay prism (now in the British Museum) recording the attempt by Sennacherib the Assyrian king to conquer Jerusalem (710 BC): Sennacherib failed —for reasons recorded in ch 36

God's Kingdom

The Book of Isaiah was written during the reigns of four kings of Judah, against the background of Assyrian attempts to overthrow God's Kingdom centred at Jerusalem. The early chapters pronounce doom—and hope—on Judah; but the prophet also has to deliver God's judgements ("burdens") upon nearby nations (chs 13-23). The prophecy looks forward to the restoration of the Kingdom, "a new heavens and a new earth" (65:17), when Christ will rule Israel and the world.

The Suffering Servant

Isaiah also prophesied the first coming of Jesus: he is referred to as Immanuel (7:14); the Son of God (9:6); the Suffering Servant (42:1-3; 52:13,14); the Lamb led to the slaughter (53:7), a Saviour who was to suffer and die, in order to conquer sin. The second half of the book (chs 40-66) opens with the words, "Comfort ye, comfort ye my people, saith your God", and brings hope of salvation not only to Jews but also Gentiles (42:6; 60:3 etc.). Ch 53 contains a moving description, written 800 years in advance, of the sufferings of the Messiah—a vivid prophecy of what actually happened to the Lord Jesus Christ.

The book concludes with descriptions of the glory of Jerusalem in the kingdom age (ch 62), and God's promise of a "new heavens and a new earth" (65:17; 66:22).

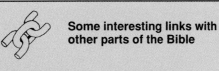

Some interesting links with other parts of the Bible

For example:

a) Isaiah 2:3

b) Isaiah 8:20

c) Isaiah 53:5

Compared with:

a) Zechariah 14:17; Matthew 5:35

b) Luke 16:29

c) Romans 5:6; 1 Peter 2:24

"For, behold, I create new heavens and a new earth: and the former shall not be remembered, nor come into mind ... The wolf and the lamb shall feed together, and the lion shall eat straw like the bullock ... They shall not hurt nor destroy in all my holy mountain, saith the LORD." (65:17,25)

JEREMIAH

God foretells the punishment of the Jews and surrounding nations for their godlessness. Israel's eventual restoration is predicted.

The Prophet of Doom

Jeremiah was directly inspired by God, like all the Old Testament prophets (see 1:9; 20:9). Though at first reluctant to speak (1:6), he foretold the overthrow of Judah and surrounding nations.

He called on the Jews not to trust in Egypt, but to submit to the Babylonians, since this was for their good!

The Suffering Prophet

For preaching such a message, Jeremiah was cast into a muddy dungeon and left to die (38:6). He was rescued and lived to see some of the events he had predicted. His experiences pointed forward to the sufferings of Jesus Christ.

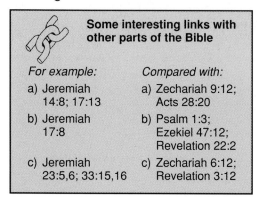

Some interesting links with other parts of the Bible

For example:
a) Jeremiah 14:8; 17:13
b) Jeremiah 17:8
c) Jeremiah 23:5,6; 33:15,16

Compared with:
a) Zechariah 9:12; Acts 28:20
b) Psalm 1:3; Ezekiel 47:12; Revelation 22:2
c) Zechariah 6:12; Revelation 3:12

The Prophet of Restoration

Jeremiah prophesied the Jews' return from Babylon after 70 years captivity (25:11,12). He also foretold their later return after centuries of scattering and persecution worldwide (see especially chs 31-33).

The Divine Potter

God speaks of Himself as being like a potter—with complete control over what He makes (18:6). He is able to mould His people into shape, if they will let Him. On the other hand, he will destroy those who become so hardened that they cannot be changed (19:11,15).

God's Prophecies Fulfilled

• After 70 years in Babylon some of the Jews returned as predicted (see Ezra 1:1; Daniel 9:2).

• In our own era, after centuries of scattering and persecution worldwide, the Jews have been returning to the Land of Israel, as was foretold.

• In 1917 the Balfour Declaration promised Palestine (then under Turkish rule) as a national homeland for the Jews.

• In 1948 the State of Israel was proclaimed; and in 1967 Jerusalem was unified as its capital city (see Luke 21:24).

TIME CHART OF THE PERIOD

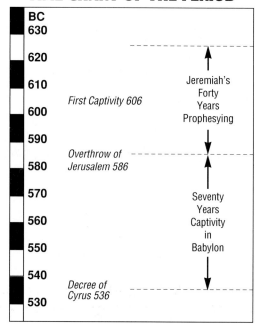

BC	
630	
620	
610	First Captivity 606 — Jeremiah's Forty Years Prophesying
600	
590	
580	Overthrow of Jerusalem 586
570	Seventy Years Captivity in Babylon
560	
550	
540	Decree of Cyrus 536
530	

"Is it nothing to you, all ye that pass by? Behold, and see if there be any sorrow like unto my sorrow!"

(1:12)

LAMENTATIONS

25

In this short Book, the Jews were told not to despise God's chastisement. The sorrows of the nation also point forward to Christ's own sufferings.

Try this Acrostic!

My 1st were those that should be close (1:2)
My 2nd, foes who were verbose (1:7)
My 3rd were troubles every day (1:7)
My 4th—those whose hand held sway (1:7)
My 5th the Jews' opponents viewed (1:8)
My 6th were pleasant—changed for food (1:11)
My 7th were just called roughly in (1:15)
My 8th refers to personal sin (1:22)
My 9th affliction sore doth know (3:1)
My 10th is how my skin doth grow (3:4)
My 11th speaks of mercies fresh (3:23)
My 12th involves no sound from flesh (3:28)
My 13th was a cry of old (3:55)
My 14th was a kind of gold (4:2)
My 15th was a gated city (4:12)
My 16th showed the Jews no pity (4:21)
My 17th asked for God to hear (5:1)
My 18th was a nation near (5:6)
My 19th Jewish females were (5:11)
My 20th—a pronoun there! (5:18)
My 21st means 'like the last' (5:21)
My 22nd—'has' (the past!) (5:22)

(The first letters of the answers make up the name of this Book—in three words)

The Desolate City

The Book of Lamentations contains a series of poems about the desolate state of the city of Jerusalem and the sufferings of the Jews. After the Babylonian invasion of 586 BC the city and the temple lay in ruins. The inspired writer (probably Jeremiah) knew that these troubles had been allowed by God because of the Jews' refusal to respond to Him. More troubles were to follow.

Despised and Rejected

The words of ch 1 are a sad commentary on the plight of the Jews, who would be despised and rejected by the world, just as God had been despised and rejected by His people.

The Man of Sorrows

The lamentations about God and His people are reflected in the sorrows and sufferings of Jesus. He "bore the yoke in his youth" (3:27) and "gave his cheek to the smiters" (3:30) for the transgressions of others (see Isaiah 53:8).

Hebrew Acrostic

The Book of Lamentations was written in an acrostic form: three of the five chapters (chs 1, 2 and 4) have 22 stanzas corresponding to the number of the letters in the Hebrew alphabet; each verse commencing with a letter of the alphabet, in order, from aleph to tau. Ch 3 has 66 shorter verses, and groups of *three* verses start with the same letter. Ch 5, though it also has 22 verses, does not follow an alphabetical pattern.

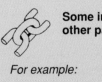

Some interesting links with other parts of the Bible

For example: | *Compared with:*

a) Lamentations 1:12 — a) Matthew 27:39; Luke 23:28

b) Lamentations 2:15 — b) Psalms 48:2; 50:2

c) Lamentations 3:30 — c) Isaiah 50:6; Matthew 26:67

The 22 letters of the Hebrew alphabet— from right to left (see also Psalm 119— section headings)

26 EZEKIEL

The obedient prophet Ezekiel is shown God's glorious purpose with Israel and surrounding nations. He sees a vision of the future Temple.

> *" And I will bring them out from the people, and gather them from the countries, and will bring them to their own land, and feed them upon the mountains of Israel " (34:13)*

Ezekiel and the Exile

Ezekiel was a priest who was taken with other Jewish captives into Babylonia about 597 BC. He was called to be God's "watchman", acting out parables and speaking "the word of the LORD" to warn God's people of the coming troubles (3:17; 33:7-9 etc.). By a vision of winged figures called "cherubim", Ezekiel was shown "the appearance of the likeness of the glory of the Lord" (1:28). He saw it "by the river of Chebar" (1:1); "in the plain" (3:23); and at Jerusalem (8:4); he saw it leaving the city (10:18; 11:23); and finally he saw the glory returning "by the way of the gate whose prospect is toward the east" (43:4).

Prophecy of Christ

God's warnings, both to Israel and to the surrounding nations, are contained in chs 3-24. Judah's last King, Zedekiah, was to be removed. There would be *no king in Israel* "until he come whose right it is" (21:27). That King will be Jesus Christ, the rightful King of the Jews!

Judgement and Restoration

Ch 37 contains a dramatic prophecy of the Valley of Dry Bones—the re-gathering of Israel, after their worldwide scattering. This process has been happening in the last hundred years. But ch 38 speaks of an invasion of Israel by "Gog, the chief prince of Meshech and Tubal ... Persia, Libya and Ethiopia with them ... Gomer ... Togarmah of the north quarters" (38:2-6). Gog's armies will be challenged by "Sheba, and Dedan, and the merchants of Tarshish" (38:13) and destroyed by God "upon the mountains of Israel" (39:4). Only the return of Christ will save Israel.

As a reassurance to the exiles, who had seen God's temple destroyed by Nebuchadnezzar, Ezekiel is granted a vision of a future Temple, to be erected at Jerusalem, a focal point for worship in the Kingdom of God, when Christ returns (chs 40-48).

Some interesting links with other parts of the Bible

For example:	Compared with:
a) Ezekiel 18:20	a) Romans 6:23
b) Ezekiel 38:15-16	b) Daniel 11:40-45
c) Ezekiel 40-48	c) Haggai 2:7-9; Micah 4:1-4

DANIEL

27

Daniel, a captive Jew in Babylon, is given visions by God about world events affecting Israel, leading to the future Kingdom of God on earth.

Nebuchadnezzar's Image

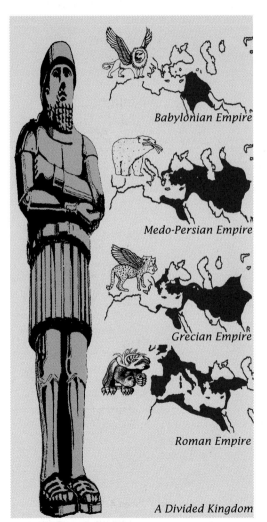

Babylonian Empire

Medo-Persian Empire

Grecian Empire

Roman Empire

A Divided Kingdom

Captives in Babylon

Daniel was a Jewish captive, taken to Babylon about 606 BC. He and his three friends, though only teenagers, displayed great courage in exile, holding to their beliefs, and worship of the true God (chs 1-3). In later years, when Daniel was about 80 years old, he faced being thrown into the lions' den, rather than give up his faith (ch 6). God delivered him; He had further work for him to perform, as His prophet.

A Book of Prophecy

The prophecies concern conflict between the kingdoms of men (particularly as they affect Israel) and the Kingdom of God.

Ch 2—*Nebuchadnezzar's Image:* the statue of a man whose parts, from head to feet, represented successive empires involved in God's purpose.

Ch 4—*Nebuchadnezzar's Dream of a Tree:* a vision concerning the future of Babylon, and the longer term Gentile period (2,520 years).

Ch 7—*Daniel's Dream of Four Beasts,* depicting the same four empires as the metals of the Image (ch 2).

Ch 8—*Daniel's Vision of the Ram and He-goat:* the future conflict of Medo-Persia and Greece, and with a longer-term prophecy centred in the "little horn".

Ch 9—*Daniel's Vision of 70 Weeks:* the period up to Messiah's coming.

Chs 10-11—*Daniel's Vision of the Kings of the North and South:* from the time of the Persians to the time of the end.

The Overthrow of Man's Rule

Ch 2, particularly, contains a dramatic forecast of the end of all human empires when a stone (Christ) topples the image and grows into God's Kingdom, centred in Israel (see 2:44). Ch 12 foretells the resurrection and judgement, and gives further time periods relevant to the last days.

Some interesting links with other parts of the Bible

For example:

a) Daniel 2:44; 7:27

b) Daniel 4:35

c) Daniel 7:2-8

Compared with:

a) Revelation 11:15

b) Isaiah 45:9; Romans 9:20,21

c) Revelation 13:1-5

28 HOSEA

A prophecy about God's love for His people, Israel. Despite her unfaithfulness, God promises to restore her and make her great.

Israel's Failure

Hosea had to warn Israel, especially the Northern Kingdom termed "Ephraim", that God would punish her, because of her disobedience.

In this Book, several symbols describe Israel's failure as God's "wife":

• Her goodness had disappeared—like a "morning cloud";

• Like a "silly dove", she had turned first to Assyria, then to Egypt, for help—instead of to God;

• She had once been like "grapes in the desert", when God first took her;

• Now she had become "like a barren fig tree" (compare Mark 11:13; Luke 21:29-31);

• She would have to plough a lone furrow, without God (see 10:11).

Israel's Future

Israel, instead of trusting in God, had tried to depend on alliances with other nations: "Ephraim hath mixed himself among the people ... strangers have devoured his strength ... they call to Egypt, they go to Assyria ... and they have not cried unto me with their heart" (7:8-14). Despite being like Hosea's own unfaithful wife (see chs 1-3), Israel would be taken back eventually (3:5; 13:14).

When God restored her, she would be like "a green fir (cypress) tree"—long lasting and upright. In that day she would bring forth fruit, to the glory of God (14:8).

> *"Come, and let us return unto the LORD: for he hath torn, and he will heal us; he hath smitten, and he will bind us up." (6:1)*

	Some interesting links with other parts of the Bible	
	For example:	*Compared with:*
	a) Hosea 1:11	a) Ezekiel 34:23,24
	b) Hosea 11:1	b) Matthew 2:15
	c) Hosea 13:14	c) 1 Corinthians 15:54,55

"Like a morning cloud ... " (6:4)

"Like a silly dove ... " (7:11)

"Once like grapes in the desert ... " (9:10)

"Now like a barren fig tree ... " (9:16)

"Like a heifer ploughing alone ... " (10:11)

JOEL

29

Forthcoming judgements in the Holy Land, including a final conflict involving all nations, when God will intervene dramatically!

"Like the noise of chariots ... like the noise of a flame of fire ... the sun and the moon shall be dark, and the stars withdraw their shining" (2:5,10)

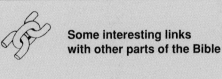

Some interesting links with other parts of the Bible

For example:

a) Joel 1:4; 2:25

b) Joel 2:27; 3:17

c) Joel 3:2

d) Joel 3:13

Compared with:

a) Deuteronomy 28:38,42

b) Ezekiel 37:26-28

c) Zechariah 14:2-4

d) Revelation 14:14-19

The Locust Plague (ch 1)

God had, from the earliest times, warned Israel that if they turned from His Word, great disasters would follow (Deuteronomy 28).

Literal plagues of locusts were sent to remind God's people of what He had said. When He appealed to the Jews through the prophet Joel, around 800 BC, God likened the forthcoming invasions of human armies to the cutting, swarming, hopping, destroying locusts, which they may already have experienced (1:4).

Invading Armies (ch 2)

Assyrian and Babylonian invasions of the land of Israel, foretold in this chapter, were followed centuries later by Greek, Roman and Mohammedan incursions. These left the Holy Land desolate until AD 1917, when the Jews were allowed to return.

Promise of Blessing (2:18-32)

The troubles which were to come on God's people had as their object the return of Israel to the true worship of God.

Great blessings are promised when this national repentance finally comes. Meanwhile, the greatest invasion of the Holy Land has yet to take place!

Final Invasion (ch 3)

Details are given of an invasion by *all* nations, at a time when Israel are back in the land (3:1), as they are today.

The wickedness of all nations is now so great (v 12-13) that when North and South become involved in a great Middle East conflict, God's judgements will be seen on the earth. The time is ripe for the putting in of His "sickle" (v 13) and the cutting down of the wicked!

God will intervene dramatically by sending Jesus Christ to Jerusalem (v 16), as so many other Scriptures indicate.

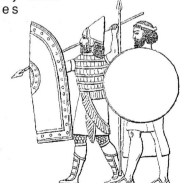

"Prepare war, wake up the mighty men" (3:9)

AMOS

30

A prophecy of troubles to come on Israel because of idolatry and immorality. Nevertheless, restoration will eventually come.

A Book of Symbols

Amos prophesied at a time (800 BC) when Israel was relatively prosperous—but when luxury and idolatry had turned the people away from their God and they were threatened by Assyrian and Babylonian invasions.

Judgements on the Nations

Amos predicted God's judgements on Syria, Philistia, Tyre, Edom, Ammon and Moab. But the prophet was also used by God to foretell His judgements on His own people—first on Israel, then on Judah. A repetition of these events can be expected in the last days, when the Middle East is again invaded from the North (see Ezekiel 35-39).

Some interesting links with other parts of the Bible

For example:	*Compared with:*
a) Amos 1:2	a) Joel 3:16
b) Amos 5:8	b) Job 38:31
c) Amos 9:14	c) Jeremiah 30:3

Various symbols are employed in this prophecy:

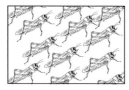

LOCUSTS (7:1-3): these symbolised the coming invasions by Assyria and Babylon (see Joel 1 & 2).

FIRE (7:4-6): indicated that the judgements would be severe—for the cleansing of Israel.

PLUMBLINE (7:7-9): Israel was not upright before God. A plumbline was needed—the Divine standard as shown later by Jesus Christ.

SUMMER FRUIT (ch 8): Just as the fruits in the basket were ripe, so Israel were ripe for judgement!

"And I will bring again the captivity of my people Israel, and they shall build the waste cities, and inhabit them; and they shall plant vineyards, and drink the wine thereof; they shall also make gardens, and eat the fruit of them. And I will plant them upon their land, and they shall no more be plucked up out of their land which I have given them, saith the LORD thy God."

(9:14,15)

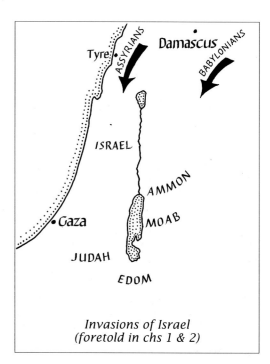

Invasions of Israel (foretold in chs 1 & 2)

OBADIAH

31

A short prophecy about Israel's Arab neighbours, which applies particularly to our days—with an amazing outcome!

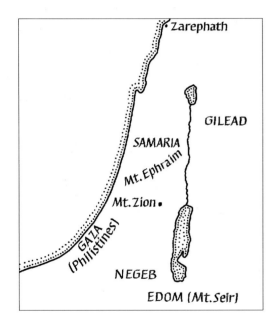

Sepharad: *The only name which is not accounted for on the map is "Sepharad" (v 20). Jewish traditions associate this with the diaspora in either Sardis (Asia Minor) or Spain. It is significant that Sepharad became the Hebrew name for Spain and gave rise to the term "Sephardic Jews"—those of Spain who in 1492 were dispersed, mostly into Mediterranean lands.*

Esau and Jacob

The name Obadiah is Hebrew, meaning 'servant of Yahweh', the God of Israel. Interestingly, this one-chapter prophecy is about both Israel and Arabs.

Those Arabs who descended from Esau (Edom) lived south and east of the Dead Sea (see map). They were always hostile to Israel, just as their ancestor Esau had been to Jacob, the ancestor of Israel (see Genesis 27:41).

When the Babylonians invaded Judah around 586 BC, the Edomites took the opportunity to stab the Jews in the back (v 11-14).

Mount Esau and Mount Zion

Mount Esau (v 8,9,19,21), sometimes called Mount Seir, is another name for the country of Edom. Today it is the southern part of the Kingdom of Jordan.

Mount Zion is at Jerusalem. Here was the capital of God's ancient Kingdom. It is here too that Christ will reign as King when he comes again!

Israel will once again occupy all that territory described in Obadiah vv 19-20. All nations, including many of the Arab peoples, will benefit when, as v 21 says, "the kingdom is the LORD's". See Isaiah 2:1-4 for details.

> *"For the day of the LORD is near upon all the nations ... But upon mount Zion shall be deliverance, and there shall be holiness; and the house of Jacob shall possess their possessions" (verses 15,17)*

Some interesting links with other parts of the Bible

For example:
a) Obadiah v 11-14
b) Obadiah v 17
c) Obadiah v 21

Compared with:
a) Psalm 137:7
b) Joel 2:32
c) Daniel 2:44; 7:27

32 JONAH

The account of how Jonah tried to escape from preaching God's word to Nineveh, and how God's Word prevailed!

Jonah's Mission

The prophet Jonah was probably the one mentioned in 2 Kings 14:25, who preached in Israel during the reign of Jeroboam II.

Israel's enemy at the time was the great Assyrian power from the north-east, with its capital at Nineveh. When God told Jonah to go and warn the Ninevites of coming judgement, he tried to escape by boarding a ship at Joppa, to flee to the far west (1:3).

However, a storm at sea prevented his escape. Thrown into the deep, Jonah was swallowed by a great fish, which God had prepared. After three days he was saved by God from this watery grave (2:10).

The Ninevites Repent

Jonah was again instructed to go and warn the Gentiles at Nineveh (3:2). The people of that great city (of 120,000 plus) repented when they heard the message from the 'risen' prophet. So God too 'repented' (ie altered His intention to punish Nineveh) (3:10).

Jonah's Reaction

The prophet's human reaction was to be displeased: he was angry that the people of Nineveh were to be spared, after all, for God had pity on them when they repented (4:11). An incident with a gourd plant, under which was shading Jonah from the sun, is used to show how God's pity for Nineveh contrasts with the prophet's impatience.

Jesus—Greater than Jonah

Some 800 years later, the one "greater than Jonah"—Jesus of Nazareth— preached to the people of Israel. But they put him to death!

Jesus had said, however, that just as Jonah was raised from his 'grave' after three days, so he too would be raised!

After his resurrection, the message Jesus had preached was to be extended to *all* nations (Mark 16:15,16). Those who would repent, believe and be baptized would be spared by God from eternal death. That message is still true for us today, no matter in what part of the world we live!

Some interesting links with other parts of the Bible

For example:

a) Jonah 1:3

b) Jonah 1:17

c) Jonah 3:10; 4:11

Compared with:

a) Acts 10:32-43

b) Matthew 12:40,41

c) 2 Peter 3:9

"He hath shewed thee, O man, what is good; and what doth the LORD require of thee, but to do justly, and to love mercy, and to walk humbly with thy God?"

(6:8)

MICAH

The prophet speaks of God's care for His people, despite their failures; His promise of a King, to be born in Bethlehem, and of a future world-wide Kingdom.

33

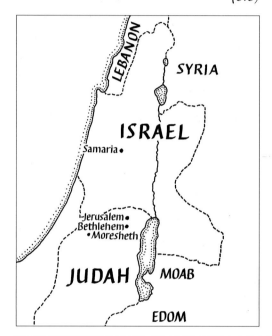

Micah of Moresheth

Micah came from south-west Judah and prophesied to the Southern Kingdom. He prophesied (as did Isaiah) during the reigns of Jotham, Ahaz and Hezekiah, kings of Judah (1:1). He spoke against idolatry, cruelty and oppression in both Judah and Israel, and warned of coming judgements.

Yet, through him, God foretold the recovery of a remnant (2:12; 5:7,8), the coming of the Messiah and the ultimate restoration of the Kingdom of God.

Summary of the Prophecy

Ch 1-3: Judgements on Samaria, Judah and Jerusalem.

Chs 4-5: Ultimate restoration under God's coming King, born in Bethlehem.

Chs 6-7: God's desire for justice, kindness and humility (6:8). He will fulfil His promise to Abraham and Jacob (7:20).

The Kingdom—Restored

The Messiah (Jesus Christ), born in David's town of Bethlehem, will be King, not only of Judah, but of the united Kingdom of Israel (see 5:2). His capital will be Jerusalem and his dominion will be worldwide. There is a wonderful description of tomorrow's world in 4:1-4 (also to be found in Isaiah 2:1-4): "Out of Zion shall go forth the law, and the word of the LORD from Jerusalem … "

A bronze coin of the Emperor Hadrian shows the ploughing of the temple area in Jerusalem by his armies, in AD 135. This event remarkably fulfilled the precise prophecy contained in Micah 3:12

Some interesting links with other parts of the Bible	
For example:	*Compared with:*
a) Micah 4:2,8	a) Obadiah 17; Isaiah 65:17-25
b) Micah 5:2	b) Matthew 2:1-6; Luke 1:32,33
c) Micah 7:20	c) Genesis 13:14-16; 28:13; 35:12

NAHUM

34

The ultimate destruction of Nineveh and the Assyrian Empire is foretold, with dramatic details of the Babylonian attack which was to come.

Background to the Book

Nahum's prophecy was a "burden against Nineveh", which can be dated between 640 and 620 BC—120 or more years after Jonah prophesied against that Assyrian city. By now Nineveh had long forgotten its repentance and had attacked and spoiled Israel, and threatened Judah. The Assyrians' attempt to overthrow Jerusalem was thwarted by divine intervention (2 Kings 19).

The Comforter

The name Nahum (like Noah) means 'comfort'. God's message through him proclaimed comfort for the Jews. Nineveh, capital of Assyria, would be overthrown and the Assyrian threat would cease for ever. The Babylonian attack on Nineveh is vividly foretold in chs 2 and 3: it was fulfilled in 612 BC. The city was finally sacked by the Medes and Persians and its ruins were only rediscovered in the 19th century.

Nineveh's Doom

Nineveh was "an exceeding great city" (Jonah 3:3). The Assyrians had conquered many nations, including Egypt: the capture of "No" (AV) or "No-Amon" (NKJV)—Thebes—on the River Nile is referred to in 3:8.

God—the Greatest!

God's words about Himself (ch 1) were right. He is in control of all nations and the judgement of Nineveh is a foreshadowing of God's final controversy with all human pride and power. Violence will not go unchecked. God will send peace to His people when Christ returns—to fulfil the words of ch 1:15.

Winged Human-headed Lion from the Palace of Nimrod at Nineveh

"Though I have afflicted thee, I will afflict thee no more. For now will I break his yoke from off thee, and will burst thy bonds in sunder" (1:12,13)

Some interesting links with other parts of the Bible

For example:

Compared with:

a) Nahum 1:2

a) Exodus 20:5; Joshua 24:19

b) Nahum 1:6

b) Malachi 3:2; Matthew 3:12

c) Nahum 1:15

c) Isaiah 52:7; Romans 10:15

HABAKKUK

35

"Write the vision; make it plain upon tablets, so he may run who reads it. For still the vision awaits its time; it hastens to the end—it will not lie" (2:2,3, RSV)

Habakkuk, concerned about Judah's troubles and Babylon's success, is allowed to see ahead to the Kingdom of God restored, when the faithful will be blessed.

God Answers a Question

Habakkuk was a prophet of God at about the time the Babylonians were attacking Judah, around 610 BC. The prophet was perplexed: Why did God appear to let wicked nations like Babylon prosper—and even be allowed to punish God's people (1:3)?

God's answer was to show him that, despite present appearances, His plan which will bring blessings for the righteous, will one day triumph: "I will work a work in your days, which ye will not believe … " (1:5).

From the watchtower on the walls of Jerusalem (2:1), the prophet was enabled to see across the centuries, to the time when the wicked will cease. Then, "The earth shall be filled with the knowledge of the glory of the LORD, as the waters cover the sea" (2:14).

A Prayer and a Song

Ch 3 contains a "prayer of Habakkuk", in the form of a song. The prophet was inspired to recall God's past triumphs, when Israel were saved from Egypt, and when they entered the Promised Land (see Deuteronomy 33:2).

Looking ahead, he saw that there will be a repeat of that victory when Christ comes, with his immortal followers, bringing fearful judgement on the wicked nations (3:16).

The Victory of Faith

Despite present troubles, those who have faith in God will be blessed when Christ returns. Those who are made "just" (or righteous) in Christ will "live" in that Day (2:4,14). So they can rejoice, even in trouble, knowing of the things in store when "he that shall come will come, and will not tarry" (2:3; Hebrews 10:37,38).

"How long O Lord?" (Habakkuk 2:1,14)

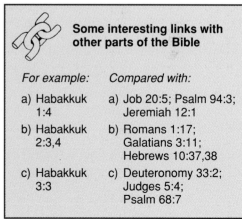

Some interesting links with other parts of the Bible

For example:	Compared with:
a) Habakkuk 1:4	a) Job 20:5; Psalm 94:3; Jeremiah 12:1
b) Habakkuk 2:3,4	b) Romans 1:17; Galatians 3:11; Hebrews 10:37,38
c) Habakkuk 3:3	c) Deuteronomy 33:2; Judges 5:4; Psalm 68:7

36 ZEPHANIAH

God warns of coming judgements on the Middle East, including the fall of Jerusalem. Nevertheless, salvation is promised for individuals who remain faithful.

Middle East Invasions

Zephaniah was a prophet of God during the reign of King Josiah over Judah, about 630 BC. Through this prophet, God warned that He would punish Israel's neighbours for their idolatry, false religion, violence and fraud (1:2,3). Judah too would be punished!

Scythians

First, God would send the Scythians. They would attack the Philistines, Moabites, the Ethiopians (Cush) and Assyrians (2:4-15) (see map).

Babylonians

Later, God would send the Babylonians against Assyria. Nineveh, its capital, would be overthrown. This was fulfilled in 612 BC. These events involving surrounding nations were to be a warning to Judah. Jerusalem itself would likewise be overthrown by the Babylonians.

Some 25 years later the Babylonian attacks on Judah began. Jerusalem was finally overthrown by Nebuchadnezzar in 586 BC and many Jews were taken into captivity.

Nevertheless, even in such troubled times, God promised ultimate salvation for the faithful.

A Rebellious People

The Jews were to be punished by God for their rebellion against Him, despite His many appeals to them (see 3:1-7). They were proud and their rulers were corrupt (3:3-5).

But not only the Jews were like that: other nations too were wicked. All were to be punished by the coming events. It still applies, that God will punish all nations for their wickedness (see 3:8).

God's Hidden Ones

The name "Zephaniah" means 'hidden of God'. Just as the faithful in those days were saved out of the fiery judgements which came on the nations, so those who today are faithful believers will be 'hidden of God' in the Day of His wrath (see 2:3 and 3:12,13).

Judgements from the North

Some interesting links with other parts of the Bible

For example: *Compared with:*

a) Zephaniah 1:15   a) Jeremiah 30:7; Joel 2:31,32

b) Zephaniah 2:3   b) Isaiah 26:20; Amos 5:15

c) Zephaniah 3:20   c) Isaiah 11:12; Jeremiah 30:3; Ezekiel 37:21

HAGGAI

37

"I will shake all nations, and the desire of all nations shall come: and I will fill this house with glory, saith the LORD of hosts." (2:7)

Haggai, with Zechariah, prophesied to the returned exiles encouraging them to complete the rebuilding of the temple and place their faith in God.

Haggai was sent by God to the Jews who had returned from captivity in Babylon. They had been led back by Zerubbabel (of royal descent) and Joshua (a High Priest). The foundations of the Temple had been laid in Jerusalem (about 535 BC), but then enthusiasm for the building waned, following opposition. Now, 18 years on, God's message through Haggai and Zechariah (see Ezra 5:1) was intended to stir the nation into action, so that He might bless them (1:1-7).

"Consider your ways!"

Not only were the returned people distracted by adversaries hindering the work, but they were becoming too comfortable: "Thus speaketh the LORD of hosts, saying,

Some interesting links with other parts of the Bible

For example:	Compared with:
a) Haggai 1:1	a) Ezra 4:24; 5:1; Zechariah 1:1
b) Haggai 1:4	b) 2 Samuel 7:2, 12-13; Psalm 132:1-5
c) Haggai 2:6,7	c) Joel 3:16-17; Hebrews 12:26-28

This people say, The time is not come, the time that the LORD's house should be built … Is it time for you, O ye, to dwell in your ceiled houses, and this house lies waste?" (1:2,4). They were warned about taking things easily, not being prepared to put any effort into the work of God, and being wasteful: "Ye have sown much, and bring in little; ye eat, but ye have not enough; ye drink, but ye are not filled with drink; ye clothe you, but there is none warm; and he that earneth wages earneth wages to put it into a bag with holes" (1:6).

They did respond: the Temple was finished in 516 BC.

Count your Blessings

When the Jews responded to God's Word through Haggai they were blessed (see Ezra 5:1-2; 7:27-28), were asked to count their blessings, and to put their faith in God's further promises.

Look Ahead!

God strengthened Zerubbabel and Joshua for the work, and helped His people. He told them to look ahead to the great King/Priest who would build an even greater "house" for God (2:6-9). This was a prophecy of the coming of Jesus Christ,

as High Priest for God's people and the future King of all nations.

The Future Temple

Haggai, and many of God's other prophets, foretold the building of a future temple at Jerusalem. It will be a focal point for the worship of the One God by all nations. See, for example, Isaiah 2:2-3; 56:7; Ezekiel 40-48; Zechariah 14:16-21.

The Royal Signet

Jesus Christ is a descendant of Zerubbabel (Luke 3:27) and is the one spoken of as God's chosen representative, having God's royal authority, appointed to rule as King of Israel and of the world (Matthew 28:18).

ZECHARIAH

At the time of Israel's return from captivity in Babylon, Zechariah is given visions relating to future events which will lead up to the Kingdom of God.

In the Reign of Darius

After the return of some of the Jews from exile in Babylon, Zechariah received prophecies from God about the future of Jerusalem and of God's people. These were given during the second and fourth years of the reign of Darius I of Persia.

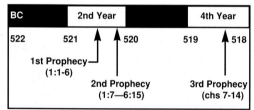

The First Prophecy

Ch 1:1-6 is a call to God's people to return to Him and to the words of His former prophets. Then He will bless them.

The Second Prophecy

Eight visions were given to Zechariah looking ahead to God's dealings with Israel:

1   The ultimate time of rest (1:7-17).
2   Four Gentile powers (Babylon, Persia, Greece, Rome) will be cut off (1:18-21).
3   Jerusalem will be restored (ch 2).
4   Arab opposition ("Satan") will be stopped (ch 3).
5   Divine Light for all nations (ch 4).
6,7   False worship will arise but will eventually be replaced (ch 5).
8   God will judge the nations when Christ rules as King/Priest (ch 6).

The Third Prophecy

Chs 7-14 fill out the message from "the LORD of hosts", whose armies fight for Israel:

ch 7   God appeals to His people to hear Him.

ch 8   He promises a future restoration (v 22,23).

ch 9   The Greek invasions of Israel and the ultimate coming of Zion's King (v 9,10).

ch 10   A second exodus of the Jews from Gentile lands is foretold.

ch 11   The Roman invasion of Israel and the cutting off of God's "shepherd" (Jesus). The uprise of false religions.

ch 12   The ultimate rescue of 'troublesome' Israel from the nations.

ch 13   The repentance of one third of Israel when they see Christ. Their ultimate salvation (v 6-8).

The golden lampstand and two olive trees (ch 4)

ch 14   The return of Christ to the Mount of Olives when "all nations are gathered against Jerusalem to battle" (v 1-4). He will rule the world (v 9). All nations will come year by year to Jerusalem to worship the LORD of hosts (v 16).

Some interesting links with other parts of the Bible

For example:

a) Zechariah 1:3,4

b) Zechariah 3:8

c) Zechariah 14:4

Compared with:

a) Jeremiah 25:4,5;
   Malachi 3:7;
   Luke 15:20,21

b) Isaiah 4:2; 11:1;
   Jeremiah 23:5; 33:15

c) Ezekiel 11:23;
   Luke 24:50,51;
   Acts 1:11,12

MALACHI

39

The old priesthood having failed, Malachi looks ahead to the coming of a better Priest who will come in judgement on the wicked, but with blessings for the faithful.

> *"The Lord, whom ye seek, shall suddenly come to his temple, even the messenger of the covenant, whom ye delight in ... But who may abide the day of his coming? and who shall stand when he appeareth?" (3:1,2)*

The Divine Messenger

Malachi (whose name means 'messenger of God') was the last of God's prophets in the Old Testament. He prophesied at about the time of Nehemiah, after the Jewish exile in Babylon. After his days "the sun went down on the prophets" for about 400 years—until the time of Jesus (see Micah 3:6).

The Message

Malachi was told to remind Israel that God had been good to them, but that priests and people alike had failed (1:2). Now their punishment must come and God would get a response from the Gentiles.

The Messenger of the Covenant

Phinehas (Numbers 25:11-13) had been a faithful priest and God had made a sure promise to him and those like him (2:5-7).

But a greater priest was to come—the Lord Jesus Christ, "the messenger of the covenant". Through him God would make a New Covenant with believers, both Jews and Gentiles. Ch 3 foretells his coming in judgement—or blessing—depending how he is received. He is to be preceded by a forerunner who will "prepare the way of the LORD" (3:1).

The Forerunner

John the Baptist was this forerunner of Jesus, preparing Israel for the Saviour (Matthew 11:10). Malachi also foretold that Elijah the prophet would come to Israel at the time of Christ's return to earth (4:5).

A Delightsome Land

When the sons of Levi are purified (3:3), God will then bless Israel. The Land of Israel will become "delightsome" (3:12) and all nations who respond will be blessed through Israel's King. Now Gentiles, too, can share in the Hope of Israel, through faith in God's promises, centred in Jesus Christ. Those who now remember the LORD and think upon His name (3:16) will be remembered by Him on that day.

My Jewels

Just as the High Priest once carried the names of the twelve tribes of Israel close to his heart, through the jewels on his breastplate (Exodus 28:29), so we can be amongst God's special treasure in the coming day (3:17).

	Some interesting links with other parts of the Bible
For example:	*Compared with:*
a) Malachi 1:11 (see 1:5, RV)	a) Isaiah 49:6; 60:3; Romans 9:24-26
b) Malachi 3:16,17	b) Exodus 28:29; Deuteronomy 4:20; 1 Peter 2:9
c) Malachi 4:2	c) Luke 1:78,79; Ephesians 5;14; Revelation 1:16

"From the rising of the sun even unto the going down of the same, my name shall be great among the Gentiles." (1:11)

"Unto you that fear my name shall the Sun of righteousness arise with healing in his wings." (4:2)

Between the Old and New Testaments

Book 39

MALACHI

Book 40

MATTHEW

The Messenger of the Covenant

The word 'testament' means a covenant. Malachi, the last of the Old Testament prophets (about 430 BC) foretold the coming of another messenger. He described him as "the messenger of the covenant", who would be preceded by one who would act as a fore-runner (Malachi 3:1).

A Long Period of Waiting

Some 430 years elapsed, during which time there were no prophets of God in Israel and no further message from Him.

The Persian Empire was succeeded by that of Alexander the Great of Greece, just as foretold earlier in the book of Daniel (see page 39). After his death, the Greek Empire was split up. North and south of the land of Israel, the Seleucids and the Ptolemies respectively held sway. The wars between Syria in the north and Egypt in the south meant a period of turbulence for the Jews situated between these two powers. This had been foretold earlier in great detail in Daniel 11.

In the Fulness of Time

The Roman Empire began to emerge about 100 BC. In Israel, a degree of independence was obtained for a while under local heroes called the Maccabees.

By the time of John the baptiser, Rome was fully in control of God's land. Nevertheless the time was ripe for the birth of the Saviour, the "messenger" of the *new* covenant. In the New Testament we read:

"When the fulness of the time was come, God sent forth his Son, made of a woman, made under the law, to redeem them that were under the law ..." (Galatians 4:4).

| 400 | 300 | 200 | 100 | BC | 0 | AD |

The World between the Testaments

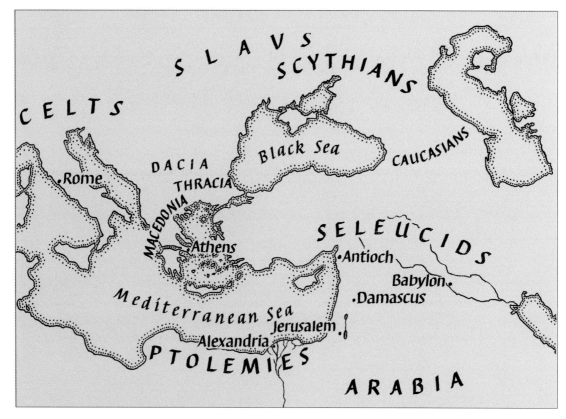

Empires rise and fall, and as the centuries pass the Jews find themselves surrounded by new neighbours. After the decline of the great empires of Egypt, Assyria, Babylon, Media and Persia, came the Greeks; then the division of Greek rule between the Seleucids and Ptolemies (with other fragments of the Greek Empire in Macedonia and Thracia); and after them the Romans. Beyond the boundaries of those empires were other migrating peoples, including Scythians, Slavs and Celts.

NEW TESTAMENT HISTORY SECTION
The Gospels and Acts

"The word which God sent unto the children of Israel, preaching good tidings of peace by Jesus Christ."

(Acts 10:36)

Books 40-44

Introduction to the GOSPELS

The Gospel writers—**Matthew**, **Mark**, **Luke** and **John**—present four views of the Lord Jesus Christ, not contradicting each other but emphasising different aspects of his life and work (see also paragraph 2 on page 58). Putting together the four records we can compile a full picture, of which the following is a very brief summary.

One or two key references are provided after each event; often the event will be found in two, three or even all four Gospels. Matthew, Mark and Luke follow a similar pattern and are sometimes called the "Synoptic Gospels".

"And there are also many other things which Jesus did, the which, if they should be written every one, I suppose that even the world itself could not contain the books that should be written."   *(John 21:25)*

Overview of the Life of Jesus

- The announcement of Jesus' birth to Mary (Matthew 1; Luke 1)
- The birth of John to Zacharias and Elisabeth (Luke 1)
- Birth of Jesus; the shepherds (Luke 2); the wise men (Matthew 2)
- The genealogy of Jesus (Matthew 1; Luke 3)
- Mary and Joseph take Jesus into Egypt (Matthew 2)
- Jesus circumcised; the testimonies of Simeon and Anna (Luke 2)
- The 12-year-old Jesus in the Temple (Luke 2)
- John the Baptist (Luke 3; 7; John 1); the baptism of Jesus (Matthew 3)
- The temptations in the wilderness (Matthew 4; Luke 4)
- Galilee: the call of the disciples (Mark 1; 2; John 1)
- The Beatitudes; Sermon on the Mount (Matthew 5-7)
- Healings and other miracles (Mark 1-11; John 2-11)
- Parables and other teachings (Matthew 13 etc.; John 2-16)
- Prayer; the Lord's Prayer (Matthew 6)
- The mission of the twelve apostles (Luke 9); the seventy (Luke 10)
- The transfiguration of Christ (Matthew 17)
- The last journey to Jerusalem (Luke 9-18)
- Entry into Jerusalem on a colt (Matthew 21; John 12)
- The Mount Olivet prophecy (Matthew 24; Mark 13; Luke 21)
- The last supper; betrayal by Judas (Matthew 26; John 13)
- Jesus' 'high-priestly' prayer (John 17)
- Gethsemane: Jesus arrested (Mark 14; John 18)
- The trial—Caiaphas, Pilate, Herod (Luke 22; 23; John 18; 19)
- Golgotha: the crucifixion (Luke 23; John 19)
- Death and burial—Joseph of Arimathea and Nicodemus (Luke 23; John 19)
- Resurrection and ascension (Luke 24; John 21)

MATTHEW

40

The first Gospel is Matthew's account of the life of Jesus, with particular emphasis on Jesus being Israel's promised Messiah and coming King.

Matthew—Tax Collector

The writer of this Gospel record was Matthew (sometimes called Levi), a tax collector working for the Romans. Such men were hated by their fellow Jews, but Jesus saw in Matthew a potential follower and called him to his service (9:9).

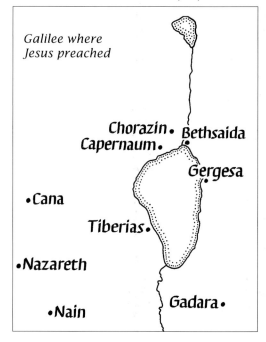

Galilee where Jesus preached

Chorazin • Bethsaida
Capernaum •
Gergesa
•Cana
Tiberias •
•Nazareth
Gadara •
•Nain

Roman Occupation

When Jesus was born in Bethlehem, and throughout his 33 years on earth, the Romans were ruling the world. An Edomite (Arab) king, Herod, ruled as the puppet head of state in Israel under the Romans.

The Jews were allowed a measure of religious freedom. But they had to pay taxes to Rome and obey Roman rule (see 17:24-27; 22:17-21 for the teaching of Jesus about obeying rulers).

The Coming King

Matthew's record from God, concerning the life and teachings of Jesus, concentrates on God's appeal to the Jews. There are abundant references to the Old Testament. Jesus is proclaimed as the "Son of David" who is to be Israel's coming King.

It is this account which tells of the search of the wise men for "him that is born King of the Jews" (2:2). It records the words of Jesus about his future Kingship (25:31). An inscription in Hebrew, Latin and Greek, "This is Jesus the King of the Jews", was placed above his head (27:37).

מלך היהודים
REX IVDAEORVM
OBACIΛEYC TWNIOYΔAIWN

Parables of the Kingdom

The parables of Jesus are featured in this Book. These simple stories were intended to instruct the faithful and confound the hard-hearted (13:13-15). Most of the parables are about the Kingdom of God and the need for us to respond to God's Word if we are to enter that Kingdom.

Some interesting links with other parts of the Bible

For example:
a) Matthew 1:1
b) Matthew 5:35
c) Matthew 16:27; 26:64

Compared with:
a) 2 Samuel 7:12-16; Romans 1:3
b) Psalm 48:2; 87:3; Isaiah 2:3
c) Psalm 110:1; Daniel 7:13; Revelation 1:7

MARK

41

Mark's inspired record of the life of Jesus, the Son of God, the one who came to heal, to serve, and to teach an urgent message.

John Mark was the son of Mary, the sister of Barnabas. He went with Paul and Barnabas on their preaching mission to Cyprus (Acts 13:4,5). He was well known to Peter who called him his "son" (1 Peter 5:13) and may have been the "young man" referred to in 14:51.

Four Views of Jesus

An interesting connection has been made between the four Gospels and the four faces of the "living creatures", or cherubim, of Ezekiel's prophecy (1:10; compare 10:14,15). Just as those faces each had the four-fold likeness of a man, a lion, an ox and an eagle, so the four Gospels, while offering a full portrait, present characteristically different views of the Lord Jesus Christ. The lion is a fitting symbol to represent Matthew's view of the 'King'; the ox corresponds to Mark's view of the 'Servant'; the human face relates to Luke's view of Christ the 'Man' (often called "Son of Man"); and the eagle is a fitting image for John's lofty portrayal of the "Son of God".

Thus Mark shows Jesus as the one who *served*. It is noteworthy how many miracles of healing and other acts of service are found in this short book:

nearly 20 are recorded in chs 1-10. It is also significant how Mark emphasises Jesus' *closeness to the people*—mingling with them, speaking personally to them, and especially touching those to whom he ministered.

Urgent News

Mark's 16 chapters are crisp and to the point! The message is simple and urgent. The last chapter gives only a brief account of the resurrection of Jesus—the vital thing was to "go into all the world and preach the gospel" (16:15).

> *"And they were beyond measure astonished, saying, He hath done all things well: he maketh even the deaf to hear, and the dumb to speak."* (7:37)

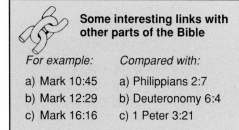

Some interesting links with other parts of the Bible

For example: Compared with:

a) Mark 10:45   a) Philippians 2:7
b) Mark 12:29   b) Deuteronomy 6:4
c) Mark 16:16   c) 1 Peter 3:21

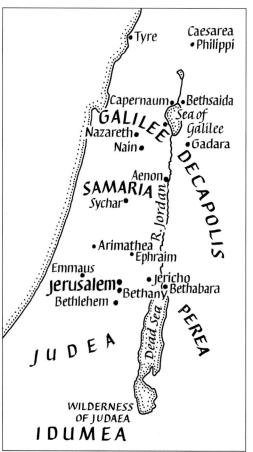

Tyre · Caesarea · Philippi

Capernaum · Bethsaida
GALILEE Sea of Galilee
Nazareth · Nain · Gadara

Aenon
SAMARIA DECAPOLIS
Sychar

· Arimathea · Ephraim
Emmaus
Jerusalem · Jericho
Bethany · Bethabara
Bethlehem ·

JUDEA Dead Sea PEREA

WILDERNESS OF JUDAEA

IDUMEA

R. Jordan

LUKE

Events in the life of Jesus, set out in order, showing him as the Son of man, the Saviour and coming King over Israel and all nations.

42

"He shall be great, and shall be called the Son of the Highest: and the Lord God shall give unto him the throne of his father David: and he shall reign over the house of Jacob for ever; and of his kingdom there shall be no end."

(1:32,33)

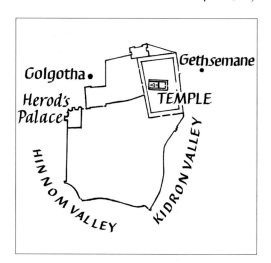

Luke's account shows the ministry of Jesus, literally and spiritually, to be a journey "up to Jerusalem"

The Birth of the Saviour

Luke, a doctor, addresses his account to the "most excellent Theophilus". He records names, places and events with meticulous care, showing Jesus as both Son of God and Son of man, descended from Adam (ch 3). His birth in Bethlehem was announced by the angels as "good tidings of great joy" to all (2:10).

Jesus was also proclaimed by an angel as the heir to the throne in Jerusalem where David once ruled (1:32,33). He will bring peace and goodwill toward men (2:14). But first Jesus had to become a Saviour from sin. Luke portrays Jesus as a man of prayer and records how he "steadfastly set his face to go to Jerusalem" and the cross (9:51; 17:11; 19:28,37,41,45).

Temple and City

Jesus foretold that the Temple and the city of Jerusalem would be overthrown— yet he would return as King in a time of "distress of nations" (21:25-28).

God's Messengers—The Angels

Note the references in Luke to angels: 1:11-19,26-38; 2:9-15; 4:10; 22:43; 24:4,23. When angels were seen they always looked like men. They did not have wings!

A Real Resurrection

The resurrection of Christ was a bodily one. Luke records some of the meetings of the risen Lord with his disciples, including his appearance to two disciples as they walked to the village of Emmaus, west of Jerusalem (24:13-35).

After his resurrection Jesus had "flesh and bones"—a real body (24:39)—and he ate with his disciples (24:41-43).

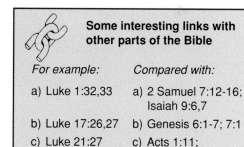

Some interesting links with other parts of the Bible

For example:	Compared with:
a) Luke 1:32,33	a) 2 Samuel 7:12-16; Isaiah 9:6,7
b) Luke 17:26,27	b) Genesis 6:1-7; 7:1
c) Luke 21:27	c) Acts 1:11; Revelation 1:7

43

JOHN

John portrays Jesus as the divine Son of God and points to the spiritual meaning of the miracles and sayings of Jesus.

"In the beginning was the Word, and the Word was with God, and the Word was God." (1:1)

The Beloved Disciple

The writer of this fourth Gospel of the Kingdom was John, brother of James, and son of Zebedee, a Galilean fisherman. Jesus called him to be one of his closest followers. He is described in this Book as "the disciple whom Jesus loved", showing how much John appreciated what Jesus stood for (13:23; 19:26; 20:2; 21:7,20).

Miracles as Signs

John focuses on certain miracles of Jesus and calls them "signs". They underline the authority Jesus had as the Son of God. They also serve as reminders of our need for healing from spiritual sickness and blindness (5:1-9; 9:1-12).

The Exalted View

God used John to reveal lofty truths about Jesus, "the word made flesh" (1:14). The exalted, soaring "eagle" aspect of Christ was noted earlier (page 58). More than any of the other evangelists (Gospel writers), John recorded the Lord's wonderful discourses on deep spiritual themes with his 'inner' group of disciples—lessons, for example, on "the bread of life", "the living water", "the good shepherd", "the true vine" (chs 6; 7; 10; 15).

> *"And many other signs truly did Jesus in the presence of his disciples, which are not written in this book: but these are written, that ye might believe that Jesus is the Christ, the Son of God; and that believing ye might have have life through his name." (John 20:30,31)*

Events in Judea

Most of John's record is concerned with events in Judea, rather than Galilee. Chs 7-11 belong to the last few weeks, and chs 12-21 to the last week of Christ's ministry!

Some interesting links with other parts of the Bible	
For example:	*Compared with:*
a) John 1:14	a) Isaiah 40:5; 2 Peter 1:17
b) John 3:14,15	b) Numbers 21:9
c) John 17:3	c) 1 Corinthians 8:6; 1 Timothy 2:5

The first of the "signs" recorded by John: changing water into wine at the wedding in Cana of Galilee (ch 2)

1st Journey ▲   ▼ *2nd Journey*

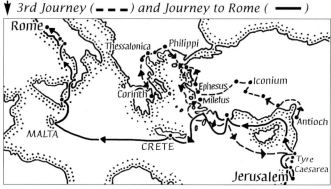

▼ *3rd Journey (– – –) and Journey to Rome (——)*

ACTS OF THE APOSTLES

44

Luke's second book, also addressed to Theophilus, records how believers in Christ separated themselves from Jewish worship and established ecclesias, starting in Judea, and spreading out into Asia Minor, Greece and finally Rome.

The Acts of Jesus ...

Luke reminds us (1:1) that he had previously written—in his gospel record—of "all that Jesus began to do and teach". After his resurrection and subsequent ascension to heaven, Jesus was still at work in the spread of the gospel.

... and his Followers

Chs 2-12 show how, with God's power (the Holy Spirit), Christ's apostles, first of all Peter and John, and then other followers such as Stephen and Philip, so effectively preached the gospel in Jerusalem, Judea and Samaria that thousands "believed and were baptized" (2:41,47; 5:14; 11:24). In Jesus' name the apostles also performed miracles.

Their message always concerned "the kingdom of God and the name of Jesus Christ" (8:12; 19:8; 28:23,31). It was a message rooted in Old Testament history and God's promises to the fathers of Israel. But it was now based on the work of Jesus Christ and not the rituals of the law of Moses. Moreover, it was a faith open to Gentiles as well as Jews.

Die-hard Jews ('Judaisers') opposed the preaching of this gospel; even among Christian converts there were some who wanted to combine their new faith in Christ with adherence to Jewish practices.

Apostle to the Gentiles

Paul, an educated Jew, had once been a zealous persecutor of Christ's followers. He was converted after seeing a vision of the risen Christ on the road to Damascus. Having believed and been baptized, he became Christ's appointed "apostle to the Gentiles" (Galatians 2:8). His three missionary journeys—preaching campaigns in Asia and Europe (see maps)—and his subsequent voyage to Rome are vividly related in chs 13 to 28.

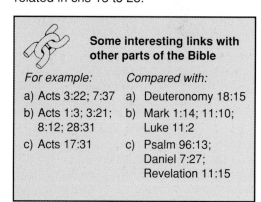

Some interesting links with other parts of the Bible

For example: *Compared with:*

a) Acts 3:22; 7:37   a) Deuteronomy 18:15

b) Acts 1:3; 3:21;   b) Mark 1:14; 11:10;
    8:12; 28:31   Luke 11:2

c) Acts 17:31   c) Psalm 96:13;
                     Daniel 7:27;
                     Revelation 11:15

Roman Provinces and Regions of the 'Diaspora'

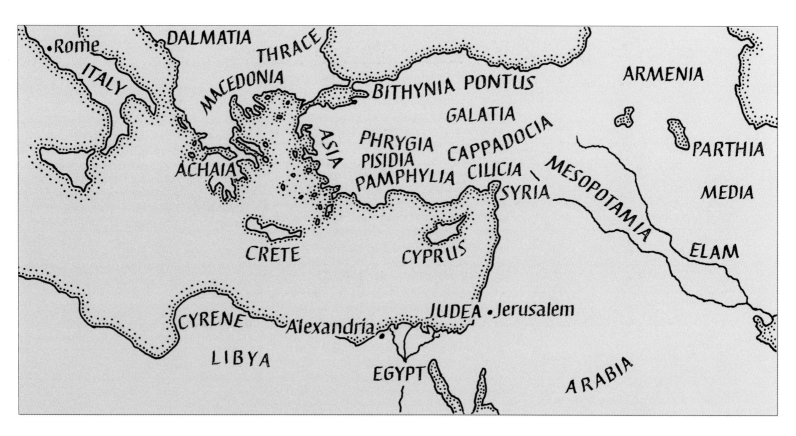

As the Gospel spread, and ecclesias were established throughout the Roman world, communication became important. The apostles wrote letters to specific ecclesias, or to groups of ecclesias: **Galatians,** for example, was sent to the group of ecclesias in Galatia; **James** was sent to Jewish believers scattered in lands of the 'Dispersion' or 'Diaspora' (James 1:1); **1 Peter** and **2 Peter** were sent to "the elect who are sojourners of the Dispersion in Pontus, Galatia, Cappadocia, Asia, and Bithynia" (1 Peter 1:1).

LETTERS SECTION

"To the saints and faithful brethren in Christ which are at ... Grace be unto you, and peace, from God our Father and the Lord Jesus Christ."

Books 45-65

Introduction to the
LETTERS SECTION

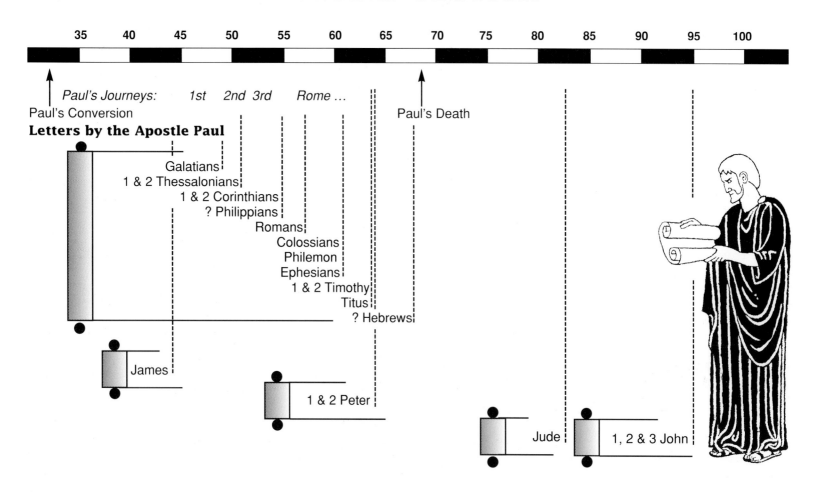

| 35 | 40 | 45 | 50 | 55 | 60 | 65 | 70 | 75 | 80 | 85 | 90 | 95 | 100 |

Paul's Journeys: 1st   2nd 3rd   Rome …

Paul's Conversion   Paul's Death

Letters by the Apostle Paul

Galatians
1 & 2 Thessalonians
1 & 2 Corinthians
? Philippians
Romans
Colossians
Philemon
Ephesians
1 & 2 Timothy
Titus
? Hebrews

James

1 & 2 Peter

Jude

1, 2 & 3 John

ROMANS

"I am not ashamed of the gospel of Christ: for it is the power of God unto salvation to every one that believeth."
(1:16)

45

Paul writes to the believers at Rome, setting out the vital principles of salvation through faith in God's promises centred in Christ.

The Believers at Rome

This letter, written with the help of Tertius on behalf of the Apostle Paul (16:22), was sent from Corinth during Paul's third missionary journey.

Paul hoped to come to Rome (15:22-29) but when he came, it was as a prisoner to await trial before the Emperor Nero (see Acts 28:17-20).

Romans is Paul's magnificent summary of the way God's righteousness is shown in the death of Christ; how salvation, by grace, is dependent on faith not works; and that it is open to Gentiles as well as Jews.

With the fulfilling of the law of Moses,

some were asking, "Hath God cast away his people?" (11:1).

With obvious emotion, Paul points out that the Jews, if they believe, are most certainly still within God's purpose—"to whom pertaineth the adoption, and the glory, and the covenants ... and the promises" (9:4). Using the symbol of an olive tree, Paul shows how some of the "natural" branches (Israel) had been broken off, and "wild shoots" (Gentiles) grafted in—but he adds that the natural branches can still be grafted in again. "Behold therefore the goodness and severity of God: on them which fell, severity; but towards thee, goodness, if thou continue in his goodness" (11:22).

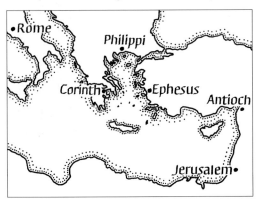

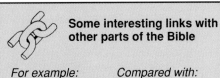

Some interesting links with other parts of the Bible

For example:	Compared with:
a) Romans 2:5-10; 14:10-12	a) 2 Corinthians 5:10; 2 Timothy 4:1
b) Romans 3:4	b) Psalm 51:4; Luke 18:19
c) Romans 6:3-4	c) Acts 22:16; Galatians 3:27

Contents of the Letter

Ch 1: Jesus "declared to be the Son of God, by the resurrection from the dead" (1:1-4). Man is "without excuse" (1:20).

Chs 2,3: All men and women are sinners in need of a Saviour, and subject to judgement, whether they are Jews or Gentiles.

Chs 4,5: Righteousness—"peace with God"—is offered to us by faith in Jesus Christ.

Chs 6-8: The new life in Christ, following adult baptism; the bondage of the Jewish Law compared with the freedom in Christ.

Chs 9-11: God chose Israel, and the covenants and promises are still associated with them; but Gentiles and Jews can now both be sharers in the same Hope.

Chs 12-15: Practical instructions for those living the new life in Christ; the problems of being surrounded by a godless world.

Ch 16
Final messages to the believers at Rome.

1 CORINTHIANS

A letter dealing with problems which had arisen at Corinth, and reminding believers of the principles which should govern God's 'household'.

Corinth ecclesia was established by Paul during his second missionary journey (see map on page 61)—there had been a warmer response to the Gospel here than in intellectual Athens. Paul wrote this whilst at Ephesus, during his third journey.

Believers with Problems

In a decadent pagan city like Corinth, it was not surprising that problems would arise: personality factions (1:12-16; 3:1-6), living in a world which boasted of its wisdom (1:17—2:16), idolatry (chs 6,8,10), doctrinal heresies (11:19), and serious moral problems (chs 5-7). The authority of the apostles was being questioned (chs 4, 9). Paul reminded the believers of the basis of their common salvation and of the need to put their house in order.

Phrases like "Now concerning ... " tell us that the letter is responding to questions which the Corinthians had raised (7:1,25; 8:1,4; 12:1; 16:1). There were misunderstandings about the memorial service ('last supper' or 'breaking of bread') (10:14-22; 11:20-29); and about 'spirit gifts' received from God (chs 12-14). Some had been given God's power (the Holy Spirit), enabling them to perform miracles, make inspired utterances, etc.

But such gifts were temporary and were to cease once the Bible had been completed (see 13:8-10). In any case, more important than gifts such as the ability to speak in tongues, or work miracles, were qualities like faith, hope and love— "and the greatest of these is love" (13:13).

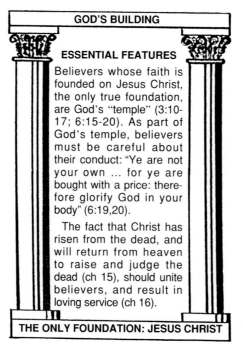

GOD'S BUILDING

ESSENTIAL FEATURES

Believers whose faith is founded on Jesus Christ, the only true foundation, are God's "temple" (3:10-17; 6:15-20). As part of God's temple, believers must be careful about their conduct: "Ye are not your own ... for ye are bought with a price: therefore glorify God in your body" (6:19,20).

The fact that Christ has risen from the dead, and will return from heaven to raise and judge the dead (ch 15), should unite believers, and result in loving service (ch 16).

THE ONLY FOUNDATION: JESUS CHRIST

"Now if Christ is preached that he has been raised from the dead, how do some among you say that there is no resurrection of the dead? But if there is no resurrection of the dead, then Christ is not risen ... And if Christ is not risen, your faith is futile; you are still in your sins! Then also those who have fallen asleep in Christ have perished. If in this life only we have hope in Christ, we are of all men the most pitiable. But now Christ has risen from the dead, and has become the firstfruits of those who have fallen asleep." (15:12,13,17-20; NKJV)

In ch 15 we have a masterly summary of the evidence for the resurrection of Jesus Christ, and clear teaching about the resurrection of faithful believers at Christ's return. The above quotation proves how essential resurrection is to the Christian Gospel.

Some interesting links with other parts of the Bible

For example:

a) 1 Corinthians 1:27

b) 1 Corinthians 3:11

c) 1 Corinthians 15:20

Compared with:

a) Psalm 8:2; Isaiah 66:2; Matthew 11:25

b) Isaiah 28:16; Ephesians 2:19-22

c) Mark 16:14; Acts 1:3; 17:31

"Be perfect ... be of one mind, live in peace; and the God of love and peace shall be with you" (13:11)

2 CORINTHIANS

47

Another letter to believers at Corinth, stressing the need to be resolute, despite all opposition, as they try to live the new life in Christ.

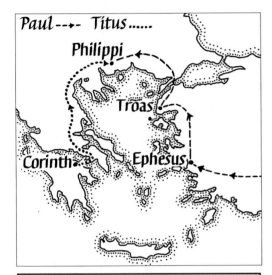

Paul --→-- Titus ......

Philippi

Troas

Corinth

Ephesus

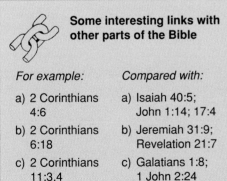

Some interesting links with other parts of the Bible

For example:

a) 2 Corinthians 4:6

b) 2 Corinthians 6:18

c) 2 Corinthians 11:3,4

Compared with:

a) Isaiah 40:5; John 1:14; 17:4

b) Jeremiah 31:9; Revelation 21:7

c) Galatians 1:8; 1 John 2:24

"I wrote with many tears"

Between the two letters to Corinth, there must have been another which has not been preserved in our Bibles—evidently even more severe in tone than the first epistle (see 2:3,4). In this 'second' letter, Paul admits his great relief that, according to news brought to Philippi by Titus (see map), the 'in-between' letter had been well received (see 7:6-15).

Though Paul is reassured about the spiritual development of the Corinthian believers, there was still much for them to learn. They had to learn that discipleship of Christ is not easy, and that all true believers must expect opposition (4:7-18).

Suffering for Christ

In Corinth, opposition would mainly come from those who had leanings towards Judaism. The 'Judaisers' would insist that believers are bound by the Law of Moses. The reader is shown that the Law was only of a *temporary* nature, whereas those things which have to do with Christ are *eternal* (see chs 3-4).

Objections by those who refused to acknowledge that Paul was a true Apostle are answered in several parts of this Letter. In ch 11, Paul defends his apostle-ship and lists some of the sufferings he had already endured for the sake of Christ.

All believers can expect persecution if they stand up for the truth. But there will be a Day of Judgement, at which true and faithful followers will be recognised by Christ (5:10).

Coin referring to Isthmian Games at Corinth (see 1 Corinthians 9:24,25)

Collection for the Needy

During his journeys, Paul collected money from the various congregations he visited, to help the poor believers in Judea. In this letter (chs 8 and 9; see also 1 Corinthians 16:1-3), he encourages the Corinthian believers to give heartily to this fund: "Every man according as he purposeth in his heart, so let him give ... for God loveth a cheerful giver" (2 Corinthians 9:7).

GALATIANS

A letter to a group of ecclesias in Asia Minor insisting that there is only one true Gospel based on God's promises to Abraham, which are inherited by faith in Christ.

Galatian 'Ecclesias'

During the 1st missionary journey Paul established a number of 'ecclesias', or assemblies, in Galatia, which was the First Century name for what is today central Turkey (see map). He visited them again on later journeys (see Acts 13-18).

The One True Gospel

Sadly, the Galatian believers were very soon influenced by Jewish elements ('Judaisers') who wanted Christians to continue observing the law of Moses. Paul reminds them of the need to keep to the one true Gospel—which no longer required rituals such as circumcision. His words still apply: "If any one is preaching to you a gospel contrary to that which you received, let him be accursed" (Galatians 1:9).

Christ or 'The Law'?

But although Jewish *practices* have been done away in Christ, the Jewish *promises*—God's covenant with Abraham in particular—are still valid. We are asked to follow the example of Abraham, the man of faith: he pleased God by *believing* Him (Genesis 15:6). We too can only be "reckoned (or accounted or credited) righteous" by *faith* in God's promises, through Christ.

Heirs of the Promises

God promised Abraham and his "seed" an eternal inheritance of the Land of Promise (Genesis 13:15). The "seed" here spoken of was Christ (3:16): by becoming associated with him, we too become heirs of the promises God made to Abraham (3:29).

Those who believe the promises and are baptized into Christ change their way of life, curbing their fleshly passions (5:15-21) and cultivating "the fruit of the Spirit" (5:22,23). They have "put on" Christ (3:27) and are thus covered by his righteousness. Paul may well have had in mind the practice of the time when a young man would 'put on' a toga—an outer garment worn by adult Romans—to mark the change to manhood.

A typical Roman toga

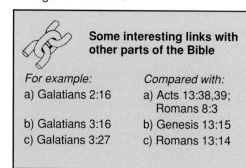 Some interesting links with other parts of the Bible	
For example:	*Compared with:*
a) Galatians 2:16	a) Acts 13:38,39; Romans 8:3
b) Galatians 3:16	b) Genesis 13:15
c) Galatians 3:27	c) Romans 13:14

EPHESIANS

An Ephesian coin showing the Temple of Diana

Paul's letter to believers at Ephesus and elsewhere, calling them to a united life in Christ, as part of God's exalted purpose.

49

Although apparently addressed to "the saints which are at Ephesus", the name of the city is omitted in some manuscripts: so this may have been a circular letter for Ephesus and other ecclesias in the vicinity.

A Holy Temple

The people worshipped idols, the most important being Diana (called Artemis by the Greeks), whose temple was at Ephesus. Followers of Christ are called to a greater Temple—formed of *believers,* both Jews and Gentiles. This Temple, when completed, will be greater than even the Jewish Temple at Jerusalem!

Built on the foundation of the teachings of God's Word, through the apostles and the prophets of the past, with Jesus Christ as "the chief corner stone", this Temple will become a dwelling-place for God Himself! (2:20-22).

The Unity of the Faith

Unity is a key theme of this Letter. The barrier between Jew and Gentile has been broken down by Christ (2:14), and all true believers have become one in him; and they are united in agreeing on the basic doctrines of their faith—summarised in 4:4-6 (and set out in the table).

Ch 5 includes a beautiful portrayal of

ONE BODY	True believers
ONE SPIRIT	God's power
ONE HOPE	Eternal life
ONE LORD	Jesus Christ
ONE FAITH	The promises
ONE BAPTISM	Adult immersion
ONE GOD	The Father

marriage, drawing out the spiritual parallel with "Christ and his church" (v 22-33).

The Armour of God

The letter gives sound practical advice on how believers are to live, putting off the "old man" and putting on "the new man" (4:22-24); by their actions they will witness to Christ.

Though raised to a high status (called "heavenly places"), they still have to fight against sin, being protected by "the whole armour of God" (6:10-17).

A Roman Soldier—Ephesus

Some interesting links with other parts of the Bible

For example:
a) Ephesians 1:22
b) Ephesians 2:8
c) Ephesians 2:12

Compared with:
a) Romans 12:5; 1 Corinthians 10:17
b) Romans 3:24; 6:23
c) Acts 11:18; John 10:16

50

PHILIPPIANS

A warm letter to a faithful ecclesia showing the need for the unity in Christ: the warfare against sin, and the ultimate joy of salvation.

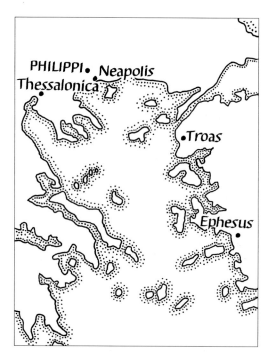

A Colony of Heaven

Philippi was a prosperous Roman colony in Thrace, at the northern end of the Aegean Sea (see map).

Here, the first "ecclesia" in Europe was established during Paul's Second Missionary Journey. Contrasting with the idea of a colony of Rome, the ecclesia is seen as a 'colony of heaven', whose members are citizens of a heavenly kingdom (see 3:20).

When he wrote this letter, Paul was a prisoner in Rome (as he had once been in Philippi, Acts 16:25). Yet he rejoices that his imprisonment had worked out "unto the furtherance of the gospel"—he was able to witness to his guards (1:12-18).

Unity in Christ

The Philippians are encouraged to "stand fast ... with one mind striving together for the faith of the gospel" (1:27). United in fellowship, "having the same love", they are "of one mind"; and they are to be concerned for each other's needs, imitating the example of Christ (2:1-5).

Though he was the Son of God, Jesus behaved as a servant and was "obedient unto death, even the death of the cross".

As a result, God raised him from the dead and has "given him a name which is above every name: that at the name of Jesus every knee should bow ... and that every tongue should confess that Jesus Christ is Lord, to the glory of God the Father" (2:6-11). Paul looked forward to the resurrection of the dead, made possible by Christ's sacrifice (3:10-12).

Think on These Things

The Philippians are to follow the example of the Lord and of the apostles (2:22,29; 3:17) and be examples to others (4:5), showing forth the qualities named in 4:8. In a city where poverty and riches existed side by side, the epistle reminds believers of the true riches of the Gospel (4:19).

> *"Finally, brethren, whatsoever things are true, whatsoever things are honourable, whatsoever things are just, whatsoever things are pure, whatsoever things are lovely, whatsoever things are of good report; if there be any virtue, and if there be any praise, think on these things." (4:8)*

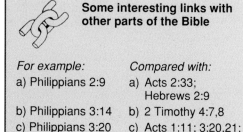

Some interesting links with other parts of the Bible

For example:	Compared with:
a) Philippians 2:9	a) Acts 2:33; Hebrews 2:9
b) Philippians 3:14	b) 2 Timothy 4:7,8
c) Philippians 3:20	c) Acts 1:11; 3:20,21; 1 Thessalonians 4:16

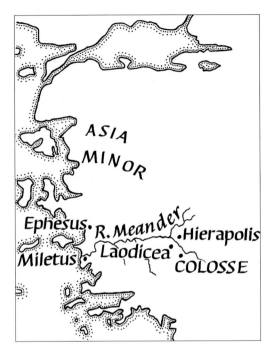

COLOSSIANS

Paul counters heresies appearing amongst the believers at Colosse. He shows that neither Judaism, nor philosophy, can save; but only commitment to Christ.

The Ecclesia at Colosse

When Paul spent three years at Ephesus (Acts 20), the Gospel spread inland to such towns as Laodicea and Colosse (see map).

While Paul was a prisoner in Rome, he learned from Epaphroditus (1:7) of problems which had arisen among believers at Colosse. So he sent this Letter via Tychicus and Onesimus (4:7-9) to the "brethren in Christ" (1:2), encouraging them to "continue in the faith, grounded and settled" (1:23) and to beware of "philosophy ... after the tradition of men" (2:8).

The main problems at Colosse arose from Judaisers and Gnostics. Paul dismissed those Jews who were still preoccupied with the Law of Moses; with "meat ... drink, or in respect of a holyday", which are done away in Christ (2:16,17). He also warned against being caught up in Greek notions of angel worship (2:18).

The Head of the Body

The Letter underlines the supremacy of the Lord Jesus Christ: there are no other intermediaries between God and man, such as the gnostics had invented. God has made His Son the head of all things, the centre of His purpose (1:16). He is the "head of the body" (the ecclesia) and the first of a new creation (1:18).

We can only be saved through association with Christ. The process begins with belief and by being "buried with him in baptism" (2:12).

Risen with Christ

Baptized believers must continue to follow Christ closely; they must live the new life in Christ (3:1). This will involve "putting to death" old ideas and ways, and "putting on the new man" (3:8-14).

'Brethren in Christ' (which is what the term "Christadelphian" means) are called to heed the instructions given in chs 3 and 4, regarding the new life.

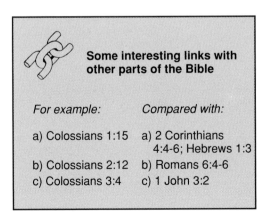

Some interesting links with other parts of the Bible

For example: *Compared with:*

a) Colossians 1:15   a) 2 Corinthians 4:4-6; Hebrews 1:3

b) Colossians 2:12   b) Romans 6:4-6

c) Colossians 3:4   c) 1 John 3:2

He is risen!

52 1 THESSALONIANS

The apostle Paul encourages and instructs believers as they await the personal return of Jesus Christ.

The Ecclesia at Thessalonica

The apostle Paul established an ecclesia of believers at Thessalonica (see map) during his Second Missionary Journey (Acts 17). The ecclesia thrived, and Paul (writing also on behalf of Silvanus and Timotheus—Silas and Timothy) says: "We give thanks to God always for you … remembering your work of faith, and labour of love, and patience of hope in our Lord Jesus Christ" (1:2,3).

Timothy had brought news of how they fared (3:6), and Paul now writes to encourage them. Using the imagery of soldiers on watch, he counsels: "Let us not sleep, but ... be sober, putting on the breastplate of faith and love; and for an helmet, the hope of salvation" (5:6-8).

The Lord will Descend

Every chapter in this book, written under Divine inspiration, forecasts the return of Christ from heaven to earth (see 1:10; 2:19; 3:13; 4:15,16; 5:2,23).

Supposing we die first?

Some believers at Thessalonica had already died, while the rest were hoping that Jesus would return at any moment. The question was being asked, "What about those who have died? Will they participate in the great events associated with his return?"

Paul explains (4:13-18) that believers are not like those who die without hope. They will be awakened from their unconscious "sleep", at the return of Christ, and will join the believers who are still living at that time. They will be caught up to meet the Lord—to be with him as he returns to the earth (not to be taken off to heaven, as believers in the 'rapture' claim). Those who are then judged by Christ to have been faithful will become his immortal helpers, to establish God's Kingdom on earth.

Some interesting links with other parts of the Bible		
For example:		Compared with:
a)	1 Thessalonians 1:10	a) Romans 5:9
b)	1 Thessalonians 2:19	b) 2 Corinthians 1:14
c)	1 Thessalonians 5:8	c) Ephesians 6:14-17

2 THESSALONIANS

53

Paul again comforts the Thessalonians, saying that Christ will come, but not before there has been a "falling away" from true religion.

Erroneous Teachings

Since the time of Christ and his apostles, error has crept into the Christian religion. The following are some of the widely held beliefs which the Bible does not support:

1. God, Jesus and the Holy Spirit form a 'trinity'.
2. Man has an 'immortal soul'.
3. Evil and temptation are the work of a supernatural 'devil'.
4. The Kingdom of God is in heaven.
5. The wicked will be punished in eternal hell-fire.
6. God has no further purpose with Israel.
7. Interpretation of Christian faith must be left to 'priests'.
8. Holy Spirit 'gifts' help believers to understand the Bible.
9. Infant sprinkling will suffice for baptism.
10. Believers can fight for their country.

Positive Bible doctrines are given, with Scripture sources, in the "Summary of Bible Teaching" on page 90.

Paul was a tent-maker: he still worked at this trade, when he could, so as not to be a burden on others (see Acts 18:3; 20:34; 1 Thessalonians 2:9)

Till Christ Comes

This letter (written, like the first, in the names of Paul, Silas and Timothy) corrected the idea that Christ would come in that era. He would come, but first there would be a "falling away" from the true teachings of Christ and his apostles (2:3). This apostasy, referred to as the "mystery of iniquity" and "the man of sin" (2:3-12), would continue down the ages until Christ comes to end it (v 8).

Stand Fast

Only the second coming of Christ, which is now imminent, can end this situation! In the meantime, the Thessalonians are praised for their devotion to the things of God, and encouraged to hold fast until the coming of the Lord!

This letter emphasises not only Christ's coming, but also the judgement: he comes "to be glorified in his saints", but also to take "vengeance on them that know not God, and that obey not the gospel of our Lord Jesus" (1:5-9).

Faith, Hope and Love

Believers can expect to suffer, but they must maintain the true Faith (beliefs) and Hope (in the coming kingdom) and show true Love, as followers of Jesus Christ (1:3; 3:5). Paul is confident that, though they have members who have been walking disorderly, they will "not be weary in well-doing"; this will bring them "peace" (3:13,16).

Some interesting links with other parts of the Bible

For example:	Compared with:
a) 2 Thessalonians 1:7-10	a) Romans 2:8,9
b) 2 Thessalonians 2:10,13	b) 1 Timothy 2:4; John 17:17
c) 2 Thessalonians 3:6	c) Romans 16:17; Titus 3:10

1 TIMOTHY

In the first of the three "Pastoral Epistles", Paul writes to Timothy, with a reminder of how affairs must be guided in the assembly of believers and of the need for sound doctrine.

"There is one God, and one mediator between God and men, the man Christ Jesus." (2:5)

Paul's "Son in the Faith"

The apostle Paul met the young man Timothy at Lystra. Timothy had a Greek father and a Jewish mother and grandmother (2 Timothy 1:5). He became a faithful helper in the work of preaching the Gospel. Paul treated him as a son (1:2), training him for the on-going work of shepherding the flock.

Timothy was entrusted with the work of guiding the believers at Ephesus, and needed advice on holding fast to the one true faith, and countering the influence of false teachers (1:3; 6:3).

The Importance of Doctrine

Paul's words to the elders of Ephesus (Acts 20:17-31) were already coming true, and "grievous wolves" were at work in the ecclesia, "not sparing the flock". The vital need for the ecclesia to keep to the original teachings of Christ and the apostles is stressed (1:3,19; 4:6,13,16; 6:3,20). Drawing on the images and language of his times, Paul uses many military, athletic and medical metaphors. He emphasises *"sound* doctrine" using a Greek word which has come down to us in the word "hygiene"—referring to what is 'wholesome' or 'healthy'. "Fight the good fight of faith"

(6:12) may sound like a military metaphor but is actually taken from athletics: the Revised English Bible translates it, "Run the great race of faith".

Another powerful expression, this time taken from the world of banking, is the "good deposit" ("that which is committed unto thee" in 6:20; "that good thing ... committed unto thee" in 2 Timothy 1:12,14). Paul tells Timothy, and us, that the faith is a precious "deposit" which we are to guard safely.

Missing the Mark

Those who taught false ideas would 'miss the mark'. This is the literal meaning of

Some interesting links with other parts of the Bible

For example:

a) 1 Timothy
   2:5; 6:15

b) 1 Timothy 6:10

c) 1 Timothy 6:16

Compared with:

a) 1 Corinthians 8:6;
   Isaiah 45:5

b) Matthew
   6:24,25,33

c) Psalm 49:12;
   Ecclesiastes 9:5

the original words used in 1:6 (translated "swerved") and 6:21 (translated "erred"; also in 2 Timothy 2:18). Some of those false teachings are dealt with in this inspired letter. For example:

1. Trinitarian ideas (1:17; 2:5; 6:15)
2. Immortal soul ideas (6:16)
3. Toleration of wrong doctrine (4:7; 5:20; 6:3,4)
4. "Science falsely so called" (6:20)

Timothy, born at Lystra, was appointed as the "bishop" (shepherd) at Ephesus

2 TIMOTHY

Paul, nearing the end of his own life, warns Timothy of perilous times ahead—both immediately, and in the last days before the return of Jesus Christ.

This letter, probably Paul's last, was written shortly before his martyrdom at the hands of the Emperor Nero in Rome, about AD 68.

Although Paul had been released after his first trial (his 'crime' was preaching the gospel!), he knew that this time his execution was imminent (see 4:6).

Final Advice

Paul had "fought a good fight" (4:7) and he urges Timothy to stand fast in the true faith, without fear (1:7; 2:1); not to be "ashamed of the testimony of our Lord, nor of me his prisoner" (1:8). Like Paul, he must be "a good soldier" for Jesus Christ (2:3).

Perilous Times

Dangers for the followers of Christ would not be confined to the First Century. Great perils would come: false teachers arose within the Christian community in those days, but the "last days" before the return of Christ would also be perilous (3:1-7). We need these warnings more than ever today.

Hope of a Future Life

Paul knew that, although man is mortal, God has offered a "promise of life" (1:1) to all true believers and a "crown of life" when Christ returns, if they have remained faithful. Paul's hope was the "crown of righteousness, which the Lord ... shall give me ... and all them also that love his appearing" (4:7,8).

"The holy scriptures are able to make thee wise unto salvation, through faith which is in Christ Jesus." (3:15)

The 'stephanos', or victor's crown, given to successful competitors in the Roman Games: "If anyone competes as an athlete, he does not receive the victor's crown unless he competes according to the rules" (2:5, NIV)

Some interesting links with other parts of the Bible

For example:
a) 2 Timothy 2:8
b) 2 Timothy 2:19
c) 2 Timothy 3:1-7

Compared with:
a) 2 Samuel 7:12-14; Luke 1:32
b) Numbers 16:5-7,26
c) Romans 1:28-31; 2 Peter 3:3,4

56

TITUS

A pastoral letter to another of Paul's "sons in the faith", who had been left to guide the ecclesias in Crete. Paul gives him instruction on how the assembly of believers should function.

Titus was a Greek and, like Timothy, seems to have been a convert of the apostle Paul. In this letter Titus is addressed as "my true child in a common faith" (Titus 1:4; compare 1 Timothy 1:2).

The "common faith" was the true Gospel, preached by the apostles. It is vital that we also hold this, as the letter says.

The Ecclesia in Crete

The assembly of believers in Crete may have been established by some who originally heard the Gospel preached by Peter at Jerusalem (see Acts 2:11). Paul's first visit to Crete was on his journey to Rome, under arrest, just before the shipwreck (Acts 27:7,8). On being released from prison in Rome he evidently visited Crete with Titus, leaving the younger man there (1:5) to "set in order" the ecclesias, "and appoint elders in every city"—there may have been many ecclesias on the island. "Unruly men, vain talkers and deceivers … heretics" (1:10; 3:10) were threatening to turn the members from the Truth. As in other places, like Galatia, the followers of Christ were in danger of being misled by "Jewish fables" (1:14).

Historically, the Cretans had gained a bad reputation. Even one of their own poets (Epimenides, 600 BC) had called them 'liars' and 'evil beasts', as Paul reminded Titus (1:12). Believers must be different, and 'bishops' (or elders) in particular should show Godly qualities and be free of the vices of the world—see 1:6-9.

Sound in the Faith

As in the letters to Timothy, Paul stresses the need for "sound doctrine" (1:9; 2:1). Believers must "hold fast to the faithful word" (1:9); they must be "sound in the faith" (1:13; 2:2), and set a good example of honesty (3:14).

All these words and phrases show how important doctrine is, as a basis for the Christian life. True beliefs and practices still matter today.

Subject to Authority

The letter to Titus exhorts slaves (of which there were many in those ecclesias) "to be obedient unto their own masters" (2:9); and all believers are "to be subject to principalities and powers" (3:1). The believer today must also respect authority.

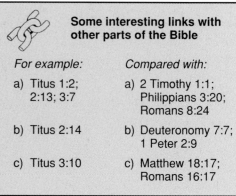

Some interesting links with other parts of the Bible

For example:	Compared with:
a) Titus 1:2; 2:13; 3:7	a) 2 Timothy 1:1; Philippians 3:20; Romans 8:24
b) Titus 2:14	b) Deuteronomy 7:7; 1 Peter 2:9
c) Titus 3:10	c) Matthew 18:17; Romans 16:17

PHILEMON

Paul's personal letter to Philemon, about Onesimus—a runaway slave who had become a believer in the true Gospel and was being commended back to his master.

> *"As Paul the aged, and now also a prisoner of Jesus Christ, I beseech thee for my son Onesimus ..." (9,10)*

Mediterranean Sea

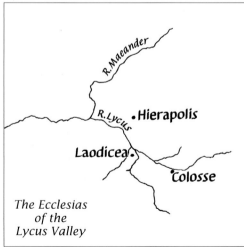

The Ecclesias of the Lycus Valley

Philemon—the Master

Philemon was a believer belonging to the ecclesia at Colosse in Asia Minor (see map). He appears to have been a wealthy man, for we know that he had at least one slave (called Onesimus).

From Rome, Paul wrote a letter to Philemon, as well as one to Colosse; from that letter to Colosse (4:8) it would appear that Tychicus was the bearer of both letters and that Onesimus accompanied him on his journey from Rome to the Lycus valley. This letter begins by commending Philemon for his faith and love towards Jesus Christ, and his kindness to the believers (v 5).

Onesimus—the Slave

But then the letter appeals to Philemon to receive back his slave, Onesimus, who had escaped and run away to Rome. Whilst in Rome, he had met Paul, who had taught him the good news of salvation in Christ. Onesimus (whose name means 'profitable') should now be received back (v 16). He had become "profitable to thee and to me" (v 11)—profitable to Paul the prisoner in Rome, to Philemon, and above all to Christ! Philemon will surely have reacted graciously to Paul's kindly letter, and will have welcomed back Onesimus—not only as a slave but also as a brother.

Who is your Master?

We are unprofitable by nature, but can be received by Christ upon our acceptance of the true Gospel. We have to be willing to obey his commands. It is far better to be a servant of Christ, that a servant of sin (see Romans 6:17). This is true freedom!

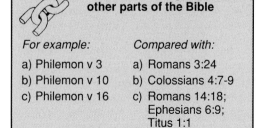

Some interesting links with other parts of the Bible	
For example:	*Compared with:*
a) Philemon v 3	a) Romans 3:24
b) Philemon v 10	b) Colossians 4:7-9
c) Philemon v 16	c) Romans 14:18; Ephesians 6:9; Titus 1:1

Paul asked Philemon to prepare him a lodging in his house (v 22)

HEBREWS

58

A letter to Jewish believers in Jerusalem, probably written by Paul, which stresses the superiority of Christ over the law of Moses and Judaism.

> *"God, who at various times and in various ways spoke in time past to the fathers by the prophets, has in these last days spoken to us by his Son."*
>
> *(1:1, NKJV)*

The Supremacy of Christ

This letter to Hebrew believers demonstrates that Jesus Christ is God's final and perfect representative, better and greater in his manifestation of God's nature and purpose than all the patriarchs, priests and prophets who preceded him. He is even greater than the angels!

Christ is greater than ...

The angels — 1:4-14
Abraham — 7:4
Moses — 3:3-6
Aaron (High Priest) — 4:14-15; 8:1-4
Joshua ("Jesus" in the AV) — 4:8
The prophets — 1:1-2

Christ—a Better Priest

The writer shows that Christ is of a higher order than the Jewish priests, who were of the tribe of Levi. Jesus was of the royal tribe of Judah, "of which tribe Moses spake nothing concerning priesthood" (7:14). But there was a precedent for this, a 'type' of Christ long before the law of Moses: Melchizedek, the king-priest of Salem (later Jerusalem) (Genesis 14:18-20). Chs 5-7 show how Christ is a "priest after the order of Melchizedek", greater than the priests who were descended from Aaron (5:6; 6:20; 7:1-21). This was foretold in one of the Psalms of David (Psalm 110:4).

Christ—Better than the Law

The Letter shows how the Law of Moses pointed forward to Christ. Ch 9 tells how he was prefigured in the Tabernacle and its contents; and in the calendar of feasts and sacrifices which Israel had to follow. And what was true for the Tabernacle, the temporary shrine in the wilderness, was also true for the Temple in Jerusalem and its rituals—which the Hebrews were reluctant to turn their backs on.

Animal sacrifices (chs 9; 10) pointed forward to a better sacrifice. Christ's sacrifice did away with the need for those sacrifices, and did away also with the need for the Temple and the priesthood.

The Way of Faith

Ch 11 shows that salvation is by faith in God's promises, centred in Jesus Christ. Jesus, though he was God's Son, was "in all points tempted like as we are, yet without sin" (2:17,18; 4:15). He is a mediator (8:6; 9:15; 12:24) for those who come in faith to ask God's forgiveness. In Jesus there is "a new and living way" (10:20); through him we may "draw near with a true heart in full assurance of faith" (10:22).

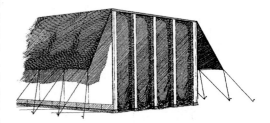

The entrance to the Tabernacle in the Wilderness

 Some interesting links with other parts of the Bible

For example:	Compared with:
a) Hebrews 2:14	a) Romans 5:21; 6:23
b) Hebrews 9:22	b) Leviticus 17:11; Matthew 26:28
c) Hebrews 13:13	c) Exodus 29:14; 33:7; Numbers 19:2,3

JAMES

59

A practical letter underlining how true brethren of Christ should both speak and act, even under conditions of stress.

"Wars and fightings" (4:1)

"Flower" (1:11)

"Ship's rudder" (3:4)

Labourers in the field (5:4)

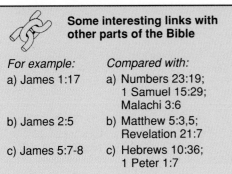

Some interesting links with other parts of the Bible

For example:	Compared with:
a) James 1:17	a) Numbers 23:19; 1 Samuel 15:29; Malachi 3:6
b) James 2:5	b) Matthew 5:3,5; Revelation 21:7
c) James 5:7-8	c) Hebrews 10:36; 1 Peter 1:7

The Lord's Brother

After Jesus, Mary had other sons, including James—the writer of this Letter. After his resurrection from the dead, Jesus appeared to his followers, who by then included his own brothers (Acts 1:14). James later became the "shepherd" of the flock of believers in the Jerusalem area (Acts 15:13).

Believers Everywhere

The Letter of James was addressed to Jewish believers further afield—those dispersed throughout the Roman world.

It was written to provide help and encouragement in the face of persecution and oppression (1:12; 5:7), but it also teaches the need to put our faith into practice. It is applicable to believers everywhere, in all ages.

Faith or Works?

From the 1st Century AD onwards, there has been debate about which is more important—faith or works. In this Letter we learn that faith (beliefs) should *result* in works (deeds); while works give *evidence* of faith. Both matter!

James gives examples of believers who showed both faith and works:

Abraham (2:21-23)—believed and obeyed God

Rahab (2:25)—showed her belief by helping God's messengers

Job (5:11)—suffered patiently

Elijah (5:17)—believed, so prayed earnestly

The Mirror of the Word

There is sound practical advice about the curbing of our tongues (ch 3), on the need for humility (ch 4), and on the importance of prayer (ch 5). If we see ourselves as we really are, by looking into God's Word, and then do nothing about it, we shall not be blessed! See what James says (1:22-25) about this "mirror".

*"If any one be a hearer of the word, and not a doer, he is like unto a man beholding his natural face in a **mirror** ... he goeth his way, and straightway forgetteth what manner of man he was" (1:23,24)*

60

1 PETER

Writing to Jewish believers among the 'diaspora', Peter proclaims Christ as the Chief Shepherd. True followers must also be shepherds, caring for the flock.

Exiles for Christ

This letter was written to Jewish believers scattered across Syria and Asia Minor (1:1; see map on page 62). Jews had either been deported or had emigrated throughout the Roman world—as far afield as Babylon and Europe. Though many opposed the preaching of Jesus Christ, some responded to the Gospel. All Christ's true followers are 'exiles', looking for the future Kingdom of God. They take no part in the politics of this world; on the other hand, they submit to kings and governors so long as their commands do not conflict with the laws of Christ.

As "strangers" in this world they must maintain their faith patiently until Christ returns, when he will grant a place in God's kingdom to all who are accepted by God's grace (1:7-9). Meanwhile, they must be prepared for persecution—those to whom Peter wrote had already experienced suffering (1:6,7; 2:11-23; 4:12-19). In this they were following in the steps of their Master, who "was reviled ... suffered ... bare our sins in his own body on the tree" (2:20-24).

Chosen People

In words once used to describe Israel, the followers of Christ are called a "chosen people", a "royal priesthood" (2:9). Christ is the Chief Shepherd, who cares for the sheep, and who even died for them (2:24,25). Believers also must care for the flock, by being good examples and by feeding them with God's Word (5:2-3).

God's special people are being prepared as a "spiritual temple" in which God can eventually dwell; Christ is the corner stone of that building (2:4-8). They must endeavour to show God's ways in their lives (2:9,12).

A Crown of Glory

Those who believe in God's Word and are baptized (1:23; 3:21) will be granted an eternal crown of life when Christ comes (5:4), if they have remained faithful.

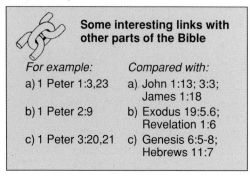

Some interesting links with other parts of the Bible

For example:

a) 1 Peter 1:3,23

b) 1 Peter 2:9

c) 1 Peter 3:20,21

Compared with:

a) John 1:13; 3:3; James 1:18

b) Exodus 19:5.6; Revelation 1:6

c) Genesis 6:5-8; Hebrews 11:7

"God waited patiently in the days of Noah while the ark was being built. In it only a few people, eight in all, were saved through water, and this water symbolises baptism that now saves you also." (3:20,21, NIV)

Echoes of the Words of Jesus

It is not difficult to see that Peter had been with Jesus Christ: dozens of phrases in this first letter can be traced to sayings of the Master. For example:

1 PETER	GOSPELS
1:4—"Inheritance ... reserved in heaven"	Matthew 6:20
1:10—"Of which salvation the prophets searched diligently ..."	Matthew 13:17
1:23—"Born again ... by the word of God"	John 3:3,5
2:5—"Ye also, as living stones, are built up a spiritual house"	Matthew 16:18
4:14—"If ye be reproached for the name of Christ, happy are ye"	Matthew 5:11
5:2—"Feed the flock of God"	John 21:16

2 PETER

61

A warning that false teachers will arise and that God will punish this dark and evil world. However, there will be great blessings for believers, when Christ returns.

The True Light

The opening verse of ch 3—"This second epistle, beloved, I now write unto you ..." (3:1)—suggests that the letter is addressed to the same readers as the first letter. Written five or six years later, it tells us that "false teachers" (2:1-3) were threatening to divert the ecclesias from the truth. In the last days, some would even deny the Second Coming of Christ (3:4).

The apostle Peter, inspired by God's Holy Spirit, proclaimed true teaching, like the prophets of God in Old Testament times (1:21). This letter, meant for believers everywhere, reminds us that God's Word of prophecy is like a lamp, shining in a squalid world (1:19), to which we need to give careful attention.

Great and Precious Promises

Peter reminds his readers of the "exceeding great and precious promises" (1:4) ... "the words spoken before by the holy prophets, and the commandment of us

the apostles of the Lord and Saviour" (3:2). Faith in these things comes first; then there must be a response (v 5-7), if one's "calling and election" is to be made sure (v 10).

Eye-Witnesses of his Majesty

Peter was one of three apostles who saw Jesus "transfigured", while they were with him on a high mountain (see Matthew 17:1-9). In this vision Jesus appeared in glorified immortal nature, as he will be seen in the future kingdom on earth.

The promise that believers might also be made "partakers of the divine nature" (1:4) had been underlined by this incident to which Peter refers (in 1:16-18).

"Where is the promise of his coming?"

Those to whom Peter wrote needed the reassurance that, though the faith was threatened by evil influences, God will judge the wicked and preserve the righteous—just as Noah was saved from the Flood (2:5), and Lot from the destruction of Sodom and Gomorrah (2:6-8).

There were some who were starting to doubt that Christ would return: "Where is the promise of his coming? for since the

fathers fell asleep, all things continue as they were from the beginning of the creation" (3:4). Peter assures them: "The Lord is not slack concerning his promise ... The day of the Lord will come as a thief in the night; in the which the heavens shall pass away ... Nevertheless we, according to his promise, look for new heavens and a new earth, wherein dwelleth righteousness" (3:10-13).

Peter and Paul

In the concluding few verses, Peter makes an interesting 'cross-reference' to Paul's epistles (3:15,16)—an incidental confirmation that the apostles knew of each other's writings.

Some interesting links with other parts of the Bible

For example:

a) 2 Peter 1:19

b) 2 Peter 1:21

c) 2 Peter 3:13

Compared with:

a) Psalms 119:105; Proverbs 6:23

b) 2 Timothy 3:16; 1 Peter 1:11

c) Isaiah 65:17; Revelation 21:1

1 JOHN

The Apostle John writes on the twin themes of Truth and Love, in opposition to the false ideas and practices which are put forward by 'antichrists'.

John's epistles were the last to be written: his gospel was probably penned in about AD 85, and these letters between 85 and 95. No recipients are named: this was a circular letter.

Fellowship with Christ

Christ was a reality in the life of the apostle John. Like others, John had seen Jesus, touched him and listened to him, both before and after his death and resurrection. John now wrote of him as "the word of life" (1:1) because belief in him and his teaching could lead to eternal life.

Fellowship "with the Father, and with his Son Jesus Christ" (1:3) is vital. We need to "walk in the light", that is, be guided by God's Word (1:6,7) if we are to have fellowship with Christ. He is the mediator through whom alone true believers can obtain forgiveness of sins (1:7; 2:2; 4:10).This blessing enables them to walk with Christ and with one another (2:1-6).

The Way of Truth

False teachings were already developing in John's day. Many were influenced by a philosophy called Gnosticism, whose followers claimed special knowledge (Greek *gnosis*), contradicting what the Christians had learned about the nature of Christ. John referred to such teachers as "antichrists" (2:18,22; 4:3). They denied that Jesus had come "in the flesh" (that is, having human nature capable of being tempted), because it was inconceivable (in their view) that one who was the Son of God could exist in human form, tainted with evil. This false idea actually paved the way for the later, unscriptural doctrine of the Trinity, which is now believed by most of Christendom.

The truth is that though God was indeed his Father, Jesus could only be a sacrifice for sin, and our "advocate with the Father" (2:1), if he shared our nature.

The Way of Love

Those who believe in the Son of God can themselves become children of God: "Behold, what manner of love the Father hath bestowed on us, that we should be called the sons of God (3:1). "God is love" (4:8) and it was because "God so loved the world" (John 3:16), that He sent His Son into the world, "that we might live through him" (4:9). Such love demands that we show love to others (3:13-23; 4:7-21).

The New Testament was written in Greek: this is a sample of text (the first few verses of John's Gospel) in the Alexandrian Manuscript (in the British Museum)

We love God when we believe His Word and keep His commandments. We love others by showing them the way of truth and eternal life (1:2; 5:20).

	Some interesting links with other parts of the Bible
For example:	*Compared with:*
a) 1 John 1:5-7	a) 2 Corinthians 6:14; 1 Thessalonians 5:5
b) 1 John 2:18	b) 2 Thessalonians 2:3; 2 Peter 2:1
c) 1 John 4:12,20	c) John 1:18; 1 Timothy 6:16

2 JOHN

63

A letter written by the apostle John, showing that those who walk in the Truth and follow its principles are God's true children.

The seconde pistle of S. Jhon

The seneour to the electe lady and her children which J love in the trueth: And not J only: but also all that have knowe the trueth, for the truthes sake, which remayneth in vs, and shal be in vs for ever.

The beginning of the Letter in Tyndale's English translation of 1525

The Beloved Elder

The apostle John was a "disciple whom Jesus loved" (John 13:23). Now, as an "elder" among the believers, he tried to guide them in the way of truth and love, as taught by Jesus.

The Elect Lady and her Children

This second epistle written by John is addressed to "the elect lady and her children" (v 1). The "lady" may have been a particular believer, but we may also think of her as the "church" or "ecclesia" as a whole.

The ecclesia consists of those who are called out by God from dying humanity to become an assembly of baptized believers. If they remain faithful they will eventually be part of the "bride" of Jesus Christ, to reign with him on earth. She will indeed be the Elect Lady; her "children" will be the individual members.

The Importance of the Truth

John was pleased to learn that the "children" were "walking in truth" (v 4). Knowing "the Truth" (the true message of God) is vital. If we do not "abide in the doctrine of Christ" (v 9), we shall not receive eternal life at his coming (v 8).

The Antichrist

In John's day (towards the end of the 1st century AD), false teaching was already being spread within the ecclesias by "many deceivers". They are called "the antichrist" (v 7). Their false ideas were the start of an apostasy which eventually affected almost the whole of Christendom.

"Receive him not"

True believers are asked to maintain the distinction between truth and error

Today false teachings still abound. For example, most 'Christians' fail to accept the Bible teaching that Jesus was of our nature—a nature from which temptation can arise. They think of him as 'God the Son' instead of the Son of God who was "tempted in all points like as we are" (Hebrews 4:15).

and not to allow false teachers to enter their "house" (or ecclesia) or to worship with them (v 10-11).

The Love of Christ

The ecclesia of Christ must continue to show true love, Divine Love, by being concerned for the eternal life of others, their fellow believers included (v 5).

Some interesting links with other parts of the Bible

For example:
a) 2 John verse 1
b) 2 John verse 6
c) 2 John verse 7

Compared with:
a) John 8:32; Galatians 1:8
b) John 14:15; 1 John 2:5
c) 2 Thessalonians 2:3,4; Acts 20:30

3 JOHN

A letter written by the Apostle John to Gaius, a beloved believer, showing our need to walk in the way of Truth and Love.

To the Beloved Gaius

The apostle John addressed this letter to "the beloved Gaius whom I love in the truth" (v 1). It may be that John had originally taught him "the Truth" (that is, the true gospel), as v 4 perhaps indicates. However, all John's fellow believers were also "beloved", having all been recipients of God's love, shown to them in Jesus Christ.

The Purpose of the Letter

John wrote asking Gaius to look after the preachers of the true gospel who were currently in his area and to attend to their needs. His letter was written under inspiration of God and so has a message for us too. Because of its personal tone and the warm love shown by the writer to the first recipient, this letter is bound to remind us of Paul's personal and affectionate letter to Philemon (see page 77).

A Good Report

Gaius was already known for his kindness. Some of the believers had reported this to the Apostle. They had confirmed also that he was following "the truth" (v 3). Strangers too had borne witness to his way of life (v 6).

Another faithful believer mentioned in this epistle was Demetrius (v 12). John wrote that he too had a good report from all men.

For us the message is clear. What we believe and how we live are both vital. If we are faithful to God's Word we too can obtain "a good report"—from God Himself (see Hebrews 11:39,40).

Self-Importance Condemned

John had previously written to the believers where Gaius lived (v 9). However, a member of the assembly there was being troublesome. His name was Diotrephes. He was a loud-mouthed man, full of his own importance. The letter shows the Divine estimate of such pride.

"No greater joy"

John rejoiced to know that most of the members walked faithfully in truth and love. If we try to live according to God's Word, this will bring joy, both to Him and to us. There is no greater joy!

Both the Second and Third Letters of John are short. Probably conscious of this, John ends each one by saying that he has more he could write about, but he will come and visit his readers instead: "I had many things to write, but I will not with ink and pen write unto thee, but I trust I shall shortly see thee, and we shall speak face to face" (v 13,14).

> Derely beloved counterfait not thatt wh/ich is evyll/but that which is good: He that do/eth well is off God: but he that doeth evyll seith not God. Demetrius hath good reporte off all men/and of the trueth. Yee and we oure selves also beare recorde/and yet knowe that oure recorde is true. J have many thynges to wryte: But J will not with pen and ynke wr/yte vnto the. For J trust J shall shortly se the/and we shall speake mouth to mouth.
> Peace be with the
> The lovers salute the.
> Grete the lovers
> by name.

The ending of the Letter in Tyndale's English New Testament

Some interesting links with other parts of the Bible

For example:	Compared with:
a) 3 John verse 4	a) 1 Corinthians 4:15; Philemon verse 10
b) 3 John verse 11	b) Psalm 37:27; Amos 5:15; 1 Peter 3:11
c) 3 John verse 12	c) Genesis 39:3; Daniel 1:9; Luke 2:52

JUDE

This short letter reminds believers that there is an urgent need always to keep to the doctrines and practices taught by Christ and the Apostles, as now revealed in the Scriptures

65

Jude, Brother of James

The writer of this letter was Jude (sometimes called Judas), the brother of the James who was a step-brother of Jesus. Jesus, Jude, James, Simon and Joses had all been brought up in the home of Mary and Joseph, at Nazareth in Galilee.

During the ministry of Jesus in Galilee, his brothers did not believe on him, although he was the Messiah and Saviour, being the Son of God and not of Joseph (see John 7:5). After his resurrection, however, they became faithful followers.

Jude, Servant of Jesus Christ

Now Jude wrote as "a servant (slave) of Jesus Christ". In writing to fellow-believers he says they are "sanctified ... preserved" (v 1). This means that they were set apart, separated and distinct from the beliefs and practices of the world around them. They will be preserved as God's people, his "saints" through Jesus Christ, if they remain true to their calling. They will look for mercy at the return of Christ if they have been faithful.

The need to contend for the faith

The ecclesia(s) to whom Jude wrote were being undermined by false teachers who had "wormed their way in" (v 4, New English Bible). Jude knew it was urgent to write and remind his readers to "earnestly contend for the faith once for all delivered unto the saints" (v 3, Revised Version). The language is very similar to 2 Peter 2.

He reminded his readers of Old Testament examples of false teachers and of the judgements reserved for such (v 5-15). Against such apostasy true saints, such as Enoch (v 14), had spoken out.

The Importance of the Truth

The need to keep to the original gospel as taught in the Scriptures is underlined in this letter. It is particularly apt, coming as it does almost at the end of the Bible. Those who guard the truth and try to live

> *"Contend earnestly for the faith which was once for all delivered unto the saints"* *(v 3)*

by its principles can look for mercy and eternal life at the time of Christ's return. They will form the faultless "Bride" to be presented in that day (v 24).

Judah, Man of Praise!

Jude's name can also be written as Judah —a name which means 'praise'. It is fitting, therefore, that the letter ends in a doxology of praise: "To the only wise God our Saviour, through Jesus Christ our Lord, be glory and majesty, dominion and power, both now and ever. Amen" (v 25).

To give God glory and praise is the ultimate purpose to which God's saints are called.

Some interesting links with other parts of the Bible

For example:

a) Jude verse 3
b) Jude verses 9,23
c) Jude verses 24,25

Compared with:

a) Philippians 1:27; 1 Timothy 6:12; 2 Timothy 1:13
b) Zechariah 3:2,4
c) Romans 16:25-27; Acts 20:32

Some New Testament People

Of several hundred names in the New Testament, a selection is given below

THOSE MARKED WITH AN ASTERISK ARE MENTIONED IN THE GOSPELS

Agrippa	Herod Agrippa II (Acts 25)	**Joseph (1)***	Husband of Mary (1)	**Peter***	Simon, an Apostle
Ananias (1)	Husband of Sapphira	**Joseph (2)***	From Arimathaea, rich man	**Philemon**	A believer at Colosse
Ananias (2)	Believer who baptized Paul	**Judas (1)***	Iscariot, the betrayer	**Philip (1)***	An Apostle from Bethsaida
Andrew*	Brother of Peter, an Apostle	**Judas (2)***	Lebbaeus, an Apostle	**Philip (2)**	A preacher, who baptized many
Anna*	Acknowledged the infant Jesus	**Jude (3)***	A 'brother' of Jesus	**Pilate***	Roman Governor of Judaea
Apollos	A believer from Alexandria	**Lazarus***	Brother of Martha and Mary; raised from the dead	**Priscilla**	Believer, wife of Aquila
Aquila	Husband of Priscilla			**Quartus**	A 'brother' (Romans 16:23)
Barnabas	Paul's companion from Cyprus	**Lebbaeus***	Thaddaeus (Judas), an Apostle	**Rhoda**	She opened the door to Peter
Bartholomew*	Nathanael, an apostle	**Luke***	He wrote 'Luke' and 'The Acts'	**Salome***	Mother of James and John
Caiaphas*	High Priest in Jerusalem	**Lydia**	She was baptized at Philippi	**Sapphira**	Wife of Ananias (1)
Cornelius	Gentile baptized by Peter	**Mark***	John Mark, who wrote 'Mark'	**Silas**	Paul's travel companion
Dorcas	Peter raised her from the dead	**Martha***	Sister of Mary (3) at Bethany	**Simeon***	Blessed the infant Jesus
Elisabeth*	Mother of John the baptist	**Mary (1)***	Mother of Jesus	**Simon (1)***	Peter, who wrote 1 & 2 Peter
Epaphroditus	Sent to Philippians by Paul	**Mary (2)***	Mother of James the 'Less'	**Simon (2)***	Zelotes, an Apostle
Felix	Roman Governor who tried Paul	**Mary (3)***	Sister of Martha and Lazarus	**Stephen**	Stoned for preaching Christ
Festus	Replaced Felix as Governor	**Mary (4)***	Magdalene, who followed Jesus	**Theophilus***	To whom Luke addressed his Gospel and Acts
Gaius	A believer with Paul at Ephesus	**Mary (5)**	Mother of John Mark		
Gamaliel	Jewish teacher of Saul (Paul)	**Mary (6)**	One of Paul's helpers at Rome	**Thomas***	Didymus, an Apostle
Herod(s)*	Puppet kings for Rome in Israel	**Mathias**	Chosen to replace Judas	**Timothy**	Young believer from Lystra
James (1)*	Brother of the Apostle John	**Matthew***	Levi, an Apostle	**Titus**	Believer sent to Crete
James (2)*	The 'Less', an Apostle	**Nicodemus***	A Pharisee who believed	**Tychicus**	Believer from Asia Minor
James (3)*	The 'brother' of Jesus	**Onesimus**	A runaway slave of Philemon	**Zacchaeus***	Tax-gatherer who was short
John (1)*	Brother of James, an Apostle	**Onesiphorus**	A believer from Ephesus	**Zacharias***	Husband of Elisabeth
John (2)*	The baptist, son of Zacharias	**Paul (Saul)**	The Apostle to the Gentiles	**Zebedee***	Father of James and John

FINAL PROPHECY SECTION

"And if any man shall take away from the words of the book of this prophecy, God shall take away his part out of the book of life, and out of the holy city, and from the things which are written in this book." (Revelation 22:19)

Book 66

Introduction to the
FINAL PROPHECY

The Prophetic Books

A very large part of the Bible is prophecy. First of all, there are the 'books of the prophets': no fewer than 17 out of the 39 books of the Old Testament. There are, in addition, those parts of other books—for example, Balaam's prophecy in Numbers, and Jesus' Mount Olivet prophecy in the Gospels—which are prophetic.

But besides those chapters or books that can be called prophecies, there are a large number of statements in other parts of the Bible which are prophetic—for example: "You will be a father of many nations" (Genesis 17:4); "I will establish the throne of his kingdom for ever" (2 Samuel 7:13).

The Purpose of Prophecy

What is the purpose of prophecy? It is usually thought of as the prediction of future events, but in fact prophecy in the Bible sense has a two-fold meaning: (1) forthtelling (speaking forth, or speaking out, on God's behalf—not necessarily predicting events); (2) foretelling (showing forth events destined to happen in the near or distant future). Isaiah, for example, writes *forthtelling* Israel's place as God's witnesses (chs 42, 43); he also *foretells* the sufferings of the Messiah (ch 53).

There are a few Bible prophecies in the form 'This or that will happen so many years from now': Jeremiah's prophecy of 70 years' captivity in Babylon (25:11) is an example. Most 'foretelling' prophecies, however, are presented in a way that makes it impossible to predict exactly when they will be fulfilled; and in relation to the events of the last days, and Christ's coming, we are clearly told that "of that day and hour knoweth no man, no, not the angels in heaven, neither the Son, but the Father" (Mark 13:32).

Foretelling future events in exact detail is, in any case, not the object of most Bible prophecies: time and again, prophecies were given so that people had an opportunity, before it was too late, to be on the look-out and to mend their ways—to make sure that they would be ready for whatever was going to happen—whenever it happened.

The Book of Revelation

When we come to the Book of Revelation, all the above principles apply. Revelation is a God-given book of prophecies about the future—"to show unto his servants things which must shortly come to pass" (1:1). It is full of symbols, including many with which we are familiar from the visions and prophecies of the Old Testament. It is given to us, not to provide precise dates for future happenings, but so that believers down the ages could be warned that cataclysmic events were about to happen, *and be ready*—and to forthtell God's involvement in them all.

Revelation may at first seem a daunting book. It often speaks in strange language; and yet, if we refer back constantly to earlier prophecies—particularly Daniel, and also the Lord's Mount Olivet prophecy—we shall begin to find meaning. In particular, many of the symbols in Old Testament prophecies—heavenly bodies, beasts, trees, etc.—reappear in the visions which John was given; and we can generally assume that such symbols have a similar significance in this final prophecy.

A Prophecy for Us

As we read the Revelation, we shall realise that this last book of prophecy, this last book of the Bible, is very relevant to our own times—and to us personally! The time is close when God shall "send Jesus Christ, who was preached unto you before, who heaven must receive until the times of restoration of all things, which God has spoken by the mouth of all His holy prophets since the world began" (Acts 3:20,21).

REVELATION

Also called the 'Apocalypse', this is a prophecy foretelling (in symbol) events leading to the return of Christ and his revelation to the world. It contains important visions of the Kingdom of God.

"The Revelation of Jesus Christ, which God gave unto him, to show unto his servants things which must shortly come to pass; and he sent and signified it by his angel unto his servant John." (1:1)

John, a Servant of Jesus Christ

The Apostle John was a prisoner on the Isle of Patmos (see map) at the end of the first century AD, when he received this prophecy. He received it directly from Jesus, and wrote it down for the benefit of Jesus' followers in all subsequent ages.

As the last of the divinely inspired writings, Revelation has many links with the first book: Genesis. The Bible begins with paradise in Eden and ends with paradise restored (Revelation 22). The prophecy is a 'revelation' or an 'uncovering' of events affecting Jesus' followers from the time of John, until Christ returns to be revealed in glory.

A Book of Symbol

It is important to note (1:1) that the book is "signified" (i.e. in symbolic form). For example, "heaven" means 'the ruling powers', and "war in heaven" refers to conflicts in human governments.

Seven-fold Visions

The number seven appears many times in the book. Seven is often used in the sense of completeness, and this is fitting as Revelation completes the Bible record. Jesus' first message is to seven churches (ecclesias) in the province of Asia, representative of his followers throughout the world (see map).

Indicating the unfolding purpose of God, there is revealed to John:

- a 7-sealed scroll—various stages in the Roman Empire until It becomes Christianised;

- 7 trumpets sounding warnings —the overthrow of the Roman power: in the West by the Barbarians, in the East by Saracens and Turks;

- 7 bowls ("vials", AV) containing plagues—aimed at the destruction of the Holy Roman Empire (West) and the Turkish Empire (East).

Visions of Glory

Each of these seven-fold sections is introduced by a vision of the coming Kingdom, to which the events move forward relentlessly and in increasing detail.

War with the Lamb

In a separate but parallel sequence, world political and religious systems are depicted as frightening beasts who make war on the Lamb—the Lord Jesus Christ—"who takes away the sin of the world" (John 1:29)

The Final Stage

The events in the prophecy lead to the overthrow of all these systems by Christ at his "revelation" (i.e. his coming) and the setting up of God's Kingdom on earth.

Some interesting links with other parts of the Bible

For example: Compared with:
a) Revelation 1:7   a) Daniel 7:13;
                         Zechariah 12:10;
                         Matthew 24:30
b) Revelation 11:15   b) Daniel 2:44; 7:27;
                         Zechariah 14:9
c) Revelation 22:18,19 c) Deuteronomy 4:2;
                         Proverbs 30:6

Summary of Bible Teaching

Theme	Teaching	Key Passages
THE BIBLE	Divinely inspired source of true teaching	Psalm 119:160; 2 Timothy 3:16,17; 2 Peter 1:20
GOD	One God, Creator, Father	Deuteronomy 6:4; John 17:3; 1 Timothy 2:5
	Holy Spirit is God's power	Genesis 1:2; Psalm 104:30; Acts 10:38
MAN	Made in the image of God	Genesis 1:26.27; 5:1; James 3:9
	Sinful, in need of redemption	Psalm 14:2,3; John 1:29; Romans 3:23
	Mortal, in need of salvation	Genesis 3:19; Ecclesiastes 9:5; John 3:16
GOD'S PURPOSE	To fill the earth with His glory	Isaiah 45:18; Habakkuk 2:14; Revelation 21:1,10,11
	To save man from sin and death	Ezekiel 18:23; Luke 2:11; 1 Timothy 2:4
JESUS CHRIST	Son of God, born to Mary	Isaiah 9:6; Matthew 1:20; Luke 1:35
	Tempted like us, but sinless	Mark 1:12,13; Hebrews 2:17; 4:15
	Crucified; raised from the dead	Matthew 28:15,16; Acts 2:23,24; 1 Corinthians 15:3,4
	Ascended to heaven; will return	Luke 24:51; Acts 1:9-11; 1 Thessalonians 4:16
KINGDOM OF GOD	Israel in the past was a prototype	2 Chronicles 9:8; Ezekiel 21:25-27; Acts 1:6; 13:22
	God's promises to Abraham concerned a land and people	Genesis 13:14-17; Acts 7:2-5; Galatians 3:29
	David was promised a descendant who would be king	2 Samuel 7:12-14; Luke 1:32; Acts 13:22,23
	Christ is the king, who will return, raise and judge the dead, and set up God's everlasting kingdom	Matthew 16:27; 1 Corinthians 15:22-24; 2 Timothy 4:1,8
	Israel will be its centre; Jerusalem its capital	Jeremiah 3:17; Micah 4:2; Matthew 5:35
SALVATION	God's plan to save man by Christ's sacrifice	Isaiah 53:4-6; Acts 4:12; 1 Timothy 1:15
	By faith, shown also in works	Genesis 15:6; Romans 10:9; James 2:14-26
	Eternal life offered to those who repent, believe and are baptized	Mark 16:16; Romans 6:4,5; Galatians 3:27-29
DISCIPLESHIP	Following Christ's standards	Romans 6:12-14; Galatians 5:22-24; 2 Peter 3:11,14
	Moral separation from the ungodly world	2 Corinthians 6:14-18; Philippians 3:20; 1 Peter 2:9

Index

Place names on maps are indicated by numbers in italics

Further Reading

The following is a small selection of leaflets and books which will help the reader to explore the Scriptures.

Helps to Bible Reading

Bible Companion (daily Bible reading calendar)
The Bible our Guide (texts supporting Bible doctrine)

Helps to Bible Study

Analytical Concordance to the Holy Bible (R. Young)
New Bible Dictionary (IVP)
Oxford Bible Atlas

Background Books by Christadelphian Authors

The Christadelphians: What they Believe and Preach (H. Tennant)
A Life of Jesus (M. Purkis)
Women of the Bible (various authors)
God's Living Word—How the Bible came to us (D. Banyard)

Other Titles in the "Study Guide" Series

Philippians Study Guide (M. G. Owen)
Song of Solomon Study Guide (S. G. Owen)
Tabernacle Study Guide (M. J. Ashton)

The above are available from the Christadelphian Office, 404 Shaftmoor Lane, Birmingham B28 8SZ, UK

Notes